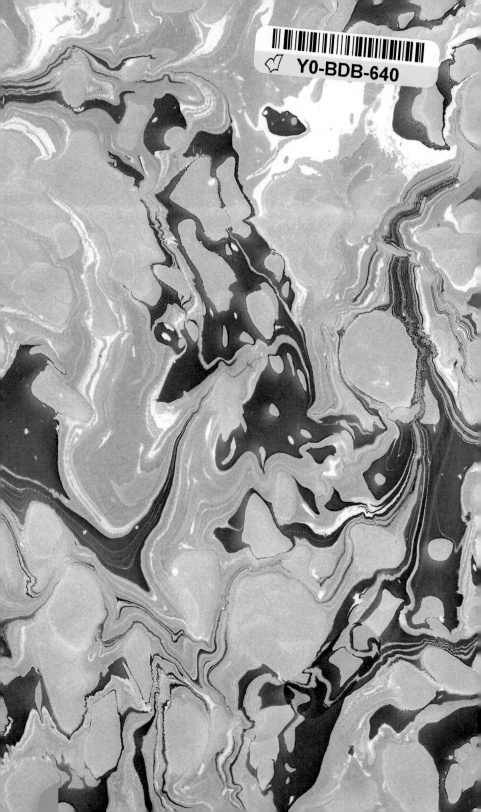

Published by ZE Books of Houston, TX
in partnership with Unnamed Press of Los Angeles, CA

3262 Westheimer Road, #467 Houston, TX 77098

www.zebooks.com

Typesetting and book design by Jaya Nicely

ISBN: 9781733540193
eISBN: 9781736309308

Library of Congress Control Number: 2021939582

Distributed by Publishers Group West

This book is a work of nonfiction.

First ZE Books Printing: August 2021

Printed in North America by McNaughton & Gunn

First Edition

2 4 6 8 9 7 5 3 1

# the skinny *a memoir*

## jonathan wells

ZE BOOKS

By its own weight, a body inclines towards its own place. Weight does not always tend towards the lowest place, but to its own place. A stone falls, but fire rises. They move according to their own weights, they seek their own places. Oil poured into water rises to the surface; water poured on oil sinks below the oil. Things out of place are restless; they find their places, and they rest.

*Pondus meum amor meus.* My love is my weight; wherever I am moved, I am moved there by love.

—Saint Augustine, *Confessions*

Now I am a little below middle stature, and this defect is not only ugly, but a disadvantage too, especially in those who hold commands and offices. For the authority conferred by a fine presence and dignity of body is lacking.

Other kinds of beauty are for the women; beauty of stature is the sole masculine beauty. When the body is small, neither a broad and domed brow, nor a clear and soft eye, nor a regular nose, nor small ears and mouth, nor white and regular teeth, nor a thick, smooth beard the color of chestnut husks, nor curly hair, nor a well-shaped head, nor a fresh complexion, nor a pleasing face, nor an odorless body, nor limbs of good proportion, will make a handsome man.

—Michel de Montaigne, "On Presumption"

## author's note

For reasons of privacy, certain names of people and places mentioned in this story have been changed.

# the skinny

*Part 1*

# chapter 1

I t was in the third week of my first year at Adams Academy, my new middle school in northern Westchester, when I learned I was thin. Not slender, as I had always thought, but as thin as a sheet of spring ice over a river. Until then, alongside my three younger siblings, my parents, aunts, uncles, cousins, and the gangly kids in my elementary school, I believed that I fit in even if it was on the lower end of the weight spectrum. Before that day no one had suggested to me that there was something wrong with me or that an intervention was needed.

The day began like the others. I stood next to my father and watched him shave. Towel tied around his waist, he steadied himself before the mirror, tilting one cheek to the light to scrape it with his razor, then the other, using torn Kleenex as his caustic. Each morning little petals of blood would blossom with white borders. I wanted to be like him, clean-cheeked, lean, and armored, as if nothing could really hurt him, so I watched every small step of his morning preparation with complete attention.

Because our house was the farthest away from school, I was picked up first by Ole, the elderly Norwegian bus driver. This gave me the chance to study his face in the rearview mirror unwatched by the other boys. Facial hair grew on Ole in places that I never saw my father touch with his razor: ears, neck, and nostrils. It grew wildly there, but he didn't appear to notice or care.

Ole barely said a word as he drove, and never looked back at us no matter how raucous and punishing the bus ride became as the other boys piled in. Instead he hissed words in a foreign language that we could tell from his menacing glances in the rearview mirror expressed his resentment of us, our rowdy behavior, and our privilege.

When the bus was filled it held ten or twelve boys dressed in button-down shirts, jackets and ties, gray slacks, and shoes with laces. Loafers were forbidden. This uniform was the junior version of Dad's uniform of suits in different shades and patterns, cuff links showing just beyond his sleeves, and wide tie with its Windsor knot. Our sports coats and slacks were more casual, more what our fathers would wear to a Saturday-night dinner party.

After half an hour of shouting, spitball blowing, and piling on the poor boy on the bottom of the curve, the bus turned into the Adams driveway. The sign was stately and could have just as gracefully been announcing a High Episcopalian church. Ole wove around the playing fields and past the estate house with its circular driveway and pillared portico, then up the final hill. We were deposited at the side entrance, where each of our names was checked on the attendance sheet as we stepped off the bus. The librarian, a woman with a prompt air about her, also made notes on our appearance. We were examined for skipped belt loops, scuffed shoes, drooping hems, and open flies. A predetermined number of dress infractions added up to demerits that could only be worked off by running quarter-mile laps around the hillside in the afternoon regardless of the weather.

We tumbled into the waxed halls and headed past the mailboxes that held school announcements for the day boys to the bulletin board for our week's assignments. When I saw that I would be sitting at Mr. McEnery's lunch table for the next two weeks, I felt a damp shiver run down my spine. As the Latin teacher at Adams, the most rigorous and conservative school in the area, he wielded an outsize influence commensurate with his physical size. He weighed at least 250 pounds, most of it protruding directly out from his midsection, and stood over six feet tall.

The teaching of Latin was at the heart of Adams culture. Its study announced that even if we boys were destined for Wall Street or big business, we weren't just traders and hagglers. Although we might acquire those skills later, they would rest on a deep foundation of learning and tradition and competitive sports. Shields steamed onto our blazers bore the school motto of *Scientia et veritas* (Knowledge and truth), and showed that we belonged to this special club.

My first classes with McEnery all began the same way. Once we had sat down, he unscrewed the top of his black fountain pen and made a check mark in his ledger next to the name of each boy who was present. Then he looked up, scanned our faces, and adjusted his striped bow tie. He picked up the stack of quizzes on his desk and thumbed through them as he stared at a fixed point over our heads. His cheeks were flushed. His forehead was high and waxy. Absentmindedly, he twirled the ends of his mustache, training them downward like Fu Manchu's. As he lifted our papers in the air, he recited, in an ethereal voice, a line from Omar Khayyam: "The Moving Finger writes; and having writ, Moves on." I sat up straight and braced myself for another poor score. "Not bad, Wells," he said as he handed it back to me. "You surprise yourself, don't you?" he said, as if it weren't a question.

At the lunch table, McEnery singled me out. From the first day, I heard that he liked to play food games on the boys at his table. He assigned me the seat opposite him at the foot of the table. As we sat down he intoned the lines from Gilbert and Sullivan, "My name is John Wellington Wells/I'm a dealer in magic and spells." But one day he added, "But your name is Jonathan, isn't it? Why Jonathan, not John? Does anyone know the difference between the two names?"

Over his half lenses he looked down the table for the brave boy who would dare to guess at the answer. He clasped his hands and rested them on his giant upturned belly. "Come on now, children. What is the difference between John and Jonathan? Someone help me, and you'll get an extra helping of dessert. Anyone?" He looked at us one by one. "All right, boys," he said. "Jonathan is a Jewish name. He was the son of Saul, king of the Israelites and forever entwined with David." As he spoke, he fluttered his lashes and looked to where the heavens would be, as if Jonathan and David's mutual ideal love was painted on the ceiling. "John is a Christian name, as you may have learned in your British history classes. Apparently, Messers Gilbert and Sullivan were not alert to the Hebraic audience, or they would have chosen to write it as 'My name is Jonathan Wells. I'm a dealer in magic and spells.' Thank you, Mr. Wells, for providing me with this opportunity to teach such an important lesson."

I watched him carefully as he started to dole out portions of chicken à la king from the vat in front of him. When it came to me he raised the spoon as if it were a sword. "Wells, feeling hungry today?" he asked with a thin smile.

"Not really," I answered. "Just a little bit, please. Thank you,"

"I'm sorry, Mr. Wells, I couldn't hear you very well. Speak up. Did you say you wanted a little more?" He dug the ladle into the bowl and dumped another scoop on my plate.

Beginning to feel my shirt stick to my back, I said, "Thank you. That's all I can eat."

"Mr. Wells, you'll have to speak louder. It is very noisy in here. I couldn't hear you. Did you say you wanted more?" Another giant spoonful landed on my plate. "Is that enough, Mr. Wells?"

"Yes, thank you," I answered. He gave me another portion or two until a mound large enough to conceal a house finch rose from it. Barely suppressing a grin, he passed the plate down the long table.

"There you go, Mr. Wells. A boy with your appetite should have no trouble polishing this off. And don't even think of leaving until you have eaten all of it. We are not here to waste food. "

The other boys looked at me with a mixture of pity and bemusement. Some smirked and cleaned their plates. I felt a kick under the table from one of the smaller boys in my class that I tried to interpret as a jolt of camaraderie. After eating the equivalent of the first helping, I paused and realized I had at least three to go.

When everyone but me had left the table, McEnery came around to visit me at my end. "This will put some padding on those bones. You are too thin, Mr. Wells. The wind could pick you up and spirit you away. And by the way, do you know why I gave you the extra helpings besides my concerns about your size?" I looked around the large dining room that was now less than a quarter full. The light streaked across the wall like a reproach.

"No I don't, Mr. McEnery."

"Well, what is the first principle of Adams Academy that we teach you on the day classes start? All teachers are always to be addressed as sir, no matter what the circumstances. You did not call me sir," he explained.

"I'm sorry, sir."

"Thank you, Mr. Wells, but it is too late for you to save your bacon. Keep eating." With that he turned on the heels of his black broken shoes that were the only flaw in his prep school teacher's attire and walked away.

I stared at my plate. I was terrified by the magnitude of the task before me. At home when I was served food I didn't like I resorted to tricks: hiding it under a lettuce leaf, covering it with a spoon. This was too much to hide. The rice had turned solid and was nearly cold. I was already full. There were hours of eating ahead of me. At this rate I would miss my afternoon classes and my soccer practice. In the windowed door of the faculty lounge I could see the smoke from McEnery's cigarette spiral around his colossal head. I was the only boy left in the dining room. All the other tables had been cleared and the chairs folded on top of them, giving the large room the feel of a prison refectory. I took another bite from time to time. The mound of food didn't move. I started forming pairs of rice kernels into groups of twins—bifurcated, damaged, and perfect specimens. The thought of the next mouthful made my gag reflex rise.

An hour later McEnery came back to check on me. The pile of food was not noticeably diminished. He stared at my plate for an extra beat and then at me as if he were weighing the seriousness of my infractions. "Mr. Wells, you may excuse yourself. Please come see me in my classroom in five minutes," he said.

The time passed slowly. I stopped in the bathroom and headed to the mirror. My eyes looked stunned open, as if I had witnessed something forbidden. I thought I could detect what he could see in me. My cheeks were sucked in; my face was mostly bone with a taut wrapping of skin. There were a few boys in my grade almost as small as I was, but they were sturdier. The rest of them were already much bigger, some by as much as a head. I straightened my tie and wet my cowlick.

When I looked through his classroom window, I saw McEnery sitting at his desk, moving his lips without a sound, the nib of his fountain pen stopped above a line of text. I walked in and he looked up at me. "Please come here, Mr. Wells," he said. I walked over to him, and he jammed one hand in each of my jacket pockets, scooped out the few coins that I'd brought to buy a candy bar from the vending machines after soccer, and laid them on his desk. "Good, Mr. Wells. I'm glad you didn't hide food in your pockets. That would call for a much harsher punishment," he said. "Do you know why I gave you so much to eat, Mr. Wells?"

"Because I didn't call you sir, sir?"

"Yes, that is one reason. Ten demerits should help you remember that in the future."

"Yes, sir."

"Because you are a mite, as in termite. A nit as in nitwit. And I am responsible for your physical as well as your intellectual growth. Please write on the board for me a hundred times, 'A word to the wise is sufficient.'"

I walked to the blackboard and began writing the phrase at the top. My shirttails came untucked as I reached up. My gray pants twisted downward on my hips as if they were being slowly unscrewed from my waist. From keeping it high in the air, my arm began to ache. My new jacket became splotched with chalk marks. I wondered if he was peeking at me secretly to see how far I had gotten, but I never caught his eyes on me. I told myself to keep writing. Don't stop. I felt as if I were on the edge of a cliff and dared not look down.

After ten more minutes at the board, I heard him say, "Mr. Wells. You can put the chalk down now. That looks close to a hundred. Come here, please." Suddenly, he smiled at me. "I don't want you to think that I am being overly harsh toward you. Nor do I want you to think that my classroom lacks jollity. Are you familiar with that word? It means we can have fun, too." Then he reached for my wrist and pulled me toward him. He squeezed me between his knees, lifted my shirt, and started tickling my left side with his index finger, the one that guided his fountain pen when he graded our papers. I was shocked by how quick he was for his size.

When he tickled me I laughed at first as though we were sharing a joke and my participation made it acceptable. But then he twisted my arm behind my back and steered me to the linoleum floor, where he held me facedown with his hand on the back of my neck. The tiles smelled as if they had just been mopped with turpentine. With my cheek pressed against them the beige and white streaks swam together. I couldn't look around to see what he was going to do next. A few seconds later he sat down on me, facing away from me as if he were riding me sidesaddle, but he was still able to tickle my side with his index finger. I couldn't see what he was doing with his other hand. My breath was heaving although I tried to get it under control. "You're not laughing, Mr. Wells. Forgive me if I'm too heavy. Who would think your little body could support my big one? We don't even know how strong we are, do we, Mr. Wells?"

I twisted my head around and saw that he wasn't laughing but beaming and panting slightly. I could only catch my breath in gasps when he changed his position to get a better seat. It felt like the wind had been knocked out of me. I was pancaked, ground into the beige mottled tiles, barely able to move and oddly weightless, as if my body no longer existed under his. I was compressed beyond thinness, almost to nothingness. McEnery intoned, "My name is Jonathan Wells. I'm a dealer in magic and spells. Well, maybe not at the moment you're not." As he repeated the lyric he kept moving his finger lightly up and down my side from my waist to my armpit. I felt shaky and my hands were trembling. I was scared imagining what he was going to do next. I had already heard about the boys who were forced to stand naked in the showers while their genitals were washed by a master who had vanished from the school.

Then for no obvious reason he rolled off me, pushed himself up, brushed invisible lint off his khaki pants, and walked back to the desk. Before he sat down he tucked his shirt back in, zipped his fly, and patted down the haywire black hairs on the top of his head. Looking into the mirror of the windows that faced the parking lot, he adjusted his bow tie. I thought I could hear him breathing in a labored way. "That'll be enough for today, Mr. Wells. You can go back to your activities now." He turned his attention to the books and papers on his desk. I felt relieved that he had stopped when he did. Even another second of his weight would have been unbearable.

I felt unstable but stood up and swiveled my pants so the fly wasn't on my hip bone, recentered my tie, and smoothed down the front of my shirt. I tried to remember what I had brought with me into his classroom and saw my notebooks had fallen underneath the chair. I picked them up and, without looking back at him, went out of his classroom and into the flow of boys in the hallways who were leaving their last classes for the large meeting hall upstairs where we sang our hymns in the morning. I found my way to my desk in the main study hall and poured my books inside.

I repeated to myself, It could have been worse, it could have been worse. I imagined myself in one of the World War II movies I loved watching with my brother Tim on the weekends. I had been grazed by a bullet but not struck dead on the spot. Surviving gave me a small surge of confidence. I kept saying that I had been sat on but not crushed, believing that the phrase might fill the indentation his weight had made in me.

I heard my name called out by the proctor from the stage: "Wells, ten demerits, insubordination." He read from a long list of boys who had committed a range of infractions from petty dress problems to cheating. After he was done, there was the standard five seconds of silence before the whole upper school, more than a hundred boys in their madras and seersucker and tweed jackets and blue blazers, stood up, shuffling their shoes as loudly as possible and banging their desktops down, filed out to go to the lockers in the gym several floors below. As I looked at them, I wondered how many others had been ridden by McEnery and how long it had taken them to recover the air in their lungs, the fullness of their bodies. Or if they ever did.

I presented myself to the demerits master at the top of the hill and began my ten laps. I ran very slowly. The trees were beginning to change color, and there were only a few clouds in the sky on that autumn day. I pushed myself up one side of the hill, floated down the other, and lingered in the shaded middle section.

During the five o'clock study hall, after I had finished my ten laps and stood lifelessly in the shower, I sat at my desk unable to concentrate. I could still feel McEnery sitting on me and the pressure on my ribs and chest. He had turned me into a hollow boy, as if I were air, empty, a rag made from a mixture of skin and clothes, the heart and joy wrung out of me.

# chapter 2

My mother was waiting for me in our green Oldsmobile station wagon at the side doors where I had been dropped off that morning, reclining in the driver's seat with her eyes closed in a relaxed meditation. Her bare arms, crossed in repose on her lap, were still tan from the summer. Her wispy blond hair was yanked back in a barrette and I could see the dark roots underneath, but they didn't diminish the soft, natural glow of her face. That gentle radiance represented maternal interest to me, but I knew it was mercurial and often fled without my noticing.

I half expected her not to be there when I walked out. Running errands spread from one Westchester town to another, she was often late, slightly frantic, and apologetic. Many times I had waited for her at the end of the piano teacher's driveway or sat alone in one of the school's outdoor chairs throwing pebbles at a tree, feeling sorry for myself when she had promised to pick me up and was half an hour or an hour late. But that day I needed her to be on time so I could climb into the refuge of her car, a haven where I knew I would be safe and receive her fullest, most sustained attention.

When I opened the door, she barely stirred. I put my school bag on the floor and tried to straighten my disheveled clothes. If there was one thing she didn't like, it was sloppiness. Especially sloppy shoes. I reached down and tied my shoelaces in a double knot. As I did, I was surprised by a voice that came from the radio. I made out the words, "young and easy...apple boughs." I closed the car door. She startled and woke up. "Oh, Jon. You're here. I'm so sorry, dear," she said, and smiled warmly. I was waiting for you and waiting, and I must have dozed off for a minute." She leaned over and put her tawny arms around my neck and pulled me toward her. She kissed the side of my head. More words from the voice: "green...carefree... famous... barns." Her arms rested on my shoulders briefly as she let the language sink through her. She pushed her driving glasses into position and shifted the car into gear.

As we drove out through the school's stone pillars, she asked, "How was your day?" in an astonished way, as if gems of knowledge might tumble out of me, nuggets of wisdom, any jewel that would distract her from the tedium of her errands.

"I learned where my name came from," I said. "From the son of a king of Israel whose name was Jonathan. He was in love with David, my teacher said." She nodded, listening more to the voice on the radio than to my answer. Who was that? I wondered. I leaned forward so I could hear the words clearly. The more fiercely I concentrated, the more McEnery was blocked from my mind. I wanted to banish every memory of him no matter how minute.

The voice continued, insistent, describing fire green as grass. What did that mean? Who was this language for? The words were in the wrong order. The colors didn't match the nouns. It seemed as if the sentences were twisted, but the cadence was unmistakable and the voice hypnotic. I wanted to trust the speaker's grave tone, but when I stopped to think about the "fire green as grass," I became as annoyed with my mother for ignoring me as with the tangled language. How could she not notice that my distress was extraordinary this time, that the disorder of my clothes was not the regular untidiness but evidence of a deeper disarray? Was she not interested in me beyond a greeting?

When the voice paused for effect, McEnery was sitting on me again. I wanted everything that had happened to me that day to spill out of me: the giant portion of food, the hours I'd spent by myself at the table chipping at the mound of rice, and McEnery with his behemoth weight on me. I wanted her to pull the car over to the side of the road so she could console me, lean her forehead against mine so I could soak up the reassurance of her voice. She was so close to me, not even six inches away. But I was afraid to ask for her attention. Maybe what McEnery had done wouldn't be interesting to her. Next to the deep, melodious voice on the cassette player mine would sound whiny and weak, so I suppressed the hurt in me and fixated on the bodiless words as if they were the only thing that could heal my pain.

As the oratory of the reader became graver, I looked out the window and pictured myself running on the demerit hillside. Well, not running. Jogging maybe. The bigger Adams rebel boys my age raced by me, taking pride in their infractions, as if the distance and exertion didn't affect them. From a distance, I had watched them sneaking cigarettes on the path down to the music barn or hiding behind the shrubbery unseen by the teacher in charge as they ran off their demerits. Their flaunting of the rules was proof that they were beyond the school's reach and whatever punishment it could mete out had no impact on them. No master was going to sit on them. I couldn't understand their defiant attitude, but I revered their invulnerability. My understanding of them never went beyond their attitude of simply not caring what happened to them. And that was a feeling I doubted I would ever have. I cared about everything.

The voice spoke of honor among foxes. If I couldn't imagine myself as one of those stronger, impervious boys, I wanted to ingratiate myself with them so I could be like them. Somehow, the voice was exhorting me to be bolder.

After the last phrase there was a pause and then Mom stopped the tape. "That was Dylan Thomas," she said. "And this poem was called 'Fern Hill.' It's his best-known one. Did you like it?"

I nodded. Even if Mom couldn't cure me herself, she had offered me the balm of this poet's language, the unfamiliar accent, the gravity of his voice, its richness, the depth of his emotion.

"I've never heard anything like that before. What country is he from?" I asked. But before my mother could answer I had to blurt out another question: "Do I weigh enough? Am I too thin? Is there something wrong with me?" She checked the rearview mirror, fiddling with her glasses on her nose as if she were stalling for time to think of an answer. Then she smiled.

"Of course not, Jon. Who told you that?"

"Nobody," I said. We continued in silence. This was the moment to tell her what McEnery had done to me, but I couldn't, although I could feel the details of the incident pushing inside me. I was afraid I might start crying and that would amount to a grand self-betrayal, so I changed the subject.

"What are we having for dinner?" I asked. There was no immediate answer, and we continued to ride along silently in the car's protective bubble.

Our house had been built on the top of a hill above the Taconic Parkway in the early 1900s. According to family legend, it had been the cancer research laboratory of a widowed doctor who had died a few years before it was abandoned. When my father bought it, it was a distressed property with potential. The first time my parents took me to visit, the sinks and vats were still attached to the wall of what would become our breakfast room. It was a forbidding place with an industrial feel that reeked of potent chemicals. Even the outside of the house with its stucco surfaces felt forbidding and unfriendly. It took two years of renovation for my mother to transform it into a comfortable family home, and we moved there as she was about to give birth to my sister, Eileen, her third child.

There were garages and toolsheds scattered around the ten-acre property, with its multiple gardens and lawns terraced into the hillside. Wooden gates, never closed, guarded the entrance to our long driveway, where a metal plaque pronounced that Nepawhin was the name of the house. My mother told me that it meant "the spirit of sleep" in Hiawatha's native language, according to Longfellow. These words gave the house a lonesome, drowsy feeling, as it towered like an improbable castle over the three-store hamlet of Millwood, which was sliced in half by derelict train tracks. On one side was Elmer's, a classic soda shop with a griddle and counter stools, and on the other a lumberyard that gave the town its name. Unlike the neighboring villages of Ossining and Chappaqua, Millwood had no ladies' or men's clothing stores or book or music shops. It was only good for a cheap hamburger and all the boards you could load on top of your station wagon.

As we pulled into the driveway, the kitchen lights glowed in the dusk beyond the rear traffic circle. I could almost see through the curtains the blue Delft tiles that my mother had chosen depicting Dutch cows and milkmaids beneath the windmills. She let me out at the back door before pulling into the garage. Bedraggled, I dragged myself up the slate steps as if my energy had been snatched by a pickpocket.

The noises of home greeted me. Marianita, our Ecuadorean cook, was in the kitchen clattering pans, trying to follow a French recipe my mother had half written out for her. My youngest brother, Danny, who was four, ran down the back hall. On seeing me, he pointed at me and singsonged, "I want to chop off your head." Then he took off again, chanting, "Chop, chop, chop off your head." He had been stuck on this chorus for weeks no matter how hard my mother tried to trick him out of it. With repetition, it became joyous and macabre and we couldn't help coaxing it out of him. I took my school bag upstairs to the room I shared with Tim, my younger brother by two years. He was sitting at his desk looking at pictures of flints that were used in the firing mechanisms of old-fashioned rifles. "What happened to you?" he said. "What took you so long to get here? I'm starving. Did you bring us anything to eat?"

"Nope. But dinner smells more American tonight."

So we could save room for the elaborate French meals that she and Marianita spent hours making, our mother forbade snacking before dinner and between meals except for raisins and celery sticks. Her enforcement of this rule was inflexible and harsh. This meant that Tim and I were so hungry by the time Dad got home from work in New York City that we would have devoured anything that was set in front of us.

Marianita had been invited by my father to join our family from her small town in the Ecuadorean Andes thanks to my cousin Gabriel's intervention. He had served two years in the Peace Corps building a schoolhouse in her village. Although she knew how to make the local maize dishes wrapped and grilled in their husks, those were not what my mother had in mind. Not one to be thwarted by language, culinary background, or inexperience my mother, who had grown up with a cook and never learned to cook herself, was determined to transform Marianita into a French chef. It was a winning if surprising partnership. My mother picked the recipes, shopped for the ingredients, and broke down the meals for her. Marianita, with Mom's constant interference, did the careful measuring that she insisted on.

We were their tasters, although little time was spent in discussion of the quality of the food. If we liked it, we ate it, and if not, we left as much as we could conceal. As soon as I reached the point of fullness, I didn't see a reason to continue, whether there was more food on my plate or not. My parents' argument of starving children in Africa didn't expand my appetite, but it did make me feel sorry for them.

Until that day at school it had never occurred to me that I was thin. I had arrived at my eating style naturally. It didn't seem different from my father's or mother's, although when there was a lull in conversation I could hear her whispering quietly to herself. Dad told us after the first time we'd noticed this that she counted each bite she took up to ten so that she would know when she reached her limit. For me, eating had never been controversial. There was no concerted pressure to eat more. When I looked around the family table I didn't think I was skinnier than my parents or my siblings. To them, beside them, I was normal. In my elementary school the teachers never mentioned that I hadn't finished what was on my tray. So what did McEnery mean about filling me up, broadening me? Compared with the other boys I may have been shorter and thinner, but people came in different sizes, didn't they? There was obviously something about my size and weight that provoked him. Again I thought of him sitting on me with horror. His smile repulsed me, and his pushing me to the floor enraged me. His words to me echoed, "Mite ... nit ... thin ... Another helping, Mr. Wells?"

To stifle what was resounding in my head I took off my jacket and tie and went downstairs to light the candles. This responsibility was a recognition of my family ranking, at the age of twelve, as the eldest child. Each night I reached inside one of the lidded brass cans for the long matchsticks. First I lit the candles in front of the antiqued mirrored sconces, trying not to catch my face there. Then I lit the taller ones in the crystal sticks on the table. After dinner was finished I reversed the order, snuffing the flames with care so that the smoke didn't blacken the silver. I took great pride in this task, so I performed it slowly and carefully, as if I were creating the light myself.

Putting the matches back, I heard the front door open and close. My father's return meant that we would be sitting down at the table soon. Even after he'd spent a day of work in the city, his black hair gleamed, slicked back on both sides of his part, and his clothes were barely creased, as if the day had had little effect on him. As he walked down the hallway, he left traces of the Old Spice aftershave he'd splashed on his cheeks that morning. The only external sign of fatigue was the exaggeration of his duck-footedness. It slowed him down as he made for the front hall table, where he set his briefcase, his brown windowpane overcoat, and his brown hat with what I thought was an owl feather tucked in its band. His arrival meant punctuality had been restored in our home. Dinner preparation in the kitchen accelerated, as though its true purpose was suddenly clear. Time, especially for my mother, stopped being movable. There was a limit to her embellishments. The moment had finally come.

Within minutes the four of us were seated. Eileen and Danny had their little kids' meal in the kitchen, fighting over whose turn it was to sit on the radiator. Then Marianita appeared through the swinging door with her good-natured smile showing its prominent gold tooth as she leaned over to serve us from the giant oval platter she carried. It was lamb chops with a parsley sauce. "Persillade" my mother called it. Dad did his best to go along with her enthusiasm for complex flavors, but whenever he was given a choice he reverted to his childhood delicacies: calves' liver, borscht, and ox tongue. With each bite of one of those dishes he clucked his tongue and wagged his head from side to side with delight.

His tastes were hard for us to acquire, as we were not born into them, and we suffered through as few bites as possible. For Mom, his foods were distasteful. They conjured a foreign life that she was removed from by at least a generation. They smacked of Russia or Poland, a shtetl life of haggard cattle, violence, scarcity, and dirt. His foods reminded him to tell us what a terrible cook his mother had been. The strongest smell in the morning when he was growing up, he said, was of burning toast. Except for that, Mom indulged him by serving his favorite dishes from time to time, but it was clear by the portions she took that she was merely observing a formality of her marriage. Her father's dairy business had its office in the Omaha slaughterhouses, so she had grown up on a diet of the freshest cuts of meat. Lox, ox tongue, smoked whitefish, and challah bread had never appeared on her dinner table.

Before Dad started on his standard dinner exercises, he turned to me and said in an indulgent tone, "I can tell something is wrong, Jon. What happened today?" Maybe Mom had alerted him that I appeared upset in the car, even if she had pretended not to notice.

"I got ten demerits and had to run them on the hillside."

"What did you do wrong?" he asked.

"I didn't call Mr. McEnery sir," I answered.

"That's it?" he asked.

"Yes," I said, "that's it."

"What kind of school is this? Reform school? Jean, you chose this place. What are they training him to be? A head waiter?" he asked, smiling slightly as if he weren't entirely displeased by the possibility. He had had as big a role in choosing Adams as she had.

"They must address all their teachers as sir or pay the price," she said. "That is the way the school is run, Arnold."

"I see," he said. "I didn't know that was still done. Not where I grew up."

With this reference we thought Dad might launch into one of his set pieces on the Depression or his boyhood in Euclid Heights, Cleveland, but that night he had another topic in mind.

"Let's say as a for instance," he began, "that the railroad industry collapsed tomorrow. No trains, no conductors, no freight, no cattle. Which businesses would be affected the most by that?" He loved giving us hypotheticals to challenge our half-formed minds.

Tim said, "Steel."

"Certainly," my father said. "What else?"

"Ball bearings?" Tim added.

"Yes, true. Jon, what's your answer?" I stared at my food.

"Food?" I asked, too tired to think further. "Agriculture. Crops?"

"Well, yes, but wouldn't trucks be able to pick up the slack?"

"I don't know if there are enough of them. And what about the workers? How would they survive?" My father, an entrepreneur whose business renting television sets in hotels and hospitals was expanding rapidly, was the son of ardent socialists who didn't believe in religion or capitalism.

"Jon found out where his Jewish name came from today," my mother announced proudly to Dad, but he didn't seem to hear her or just ignored the statement.

"How about some number exercises?" he asked. We groaned as we kept sawing through our lamb chops with the thick green sauce. At least three times a week he tested our multiplication and division skills. He turned to me and said, "Jon, take the number eighty-five, multiply by twelve, add two hundred, and divide by four. Don't think. React." I wasn't sure how I was supposed to react to numbers, as they weren't food or candy or jokes. The emphasis in these exercises was on speed, not accuracy, as he had told us many times. There was no ability more critical for his job, he swore, than to be able to perform intricate calculations in his head and reach the approximately right answer. "What have you got?" he asked, prodding me. "Take me through the steps. Eighty-five times twelve equals what?"

"Nine hundred," I answered.

"Okay, close enough. Plus two hundred is eleven hundred. Now divide by four. Ignore the nickels and pennies," he added, alluding to his hypothesis that it was only the bigger sums that mattered. The clear lesson to us was that rounding off was the key to success.

After the main course we folded our napkins and stood up to have dessert in the living room across the front hall. While we waited for it to be rolled in on the rickety glass cart, Mom put Danny and Eileen to bed while Tim and I sat down in front of the fireplace even though it was only September. Every night of the school year we went through the ritual of building the fire together. In order to avoid disputes, Tim and I were both allowed to put a match to the logs and newspapers, each at a separate end of the stack. We watched the flames for a minute or two, and then we went up to finish our homework. I glanced at my Latin textbook, but as hard as I tried, all I could picture was McEnery's classroom: the arrangement of the desks, and him sitting in his master's wooden armchair, his striped shirt with its white collar and cuffs sticking out from his blazer as if Brooks Brothers had designed a line of beach balls. His delicate, blanched fingers guided his pen as he read.

As I undressed I felt more and more morose, submerged in the memory of what McEnery had done. The shock of it led me to analytical thoughts and justifications. I hid the horror behind excuses I made on my behalf. I should have been braver. I should have resisted more. How would the Adams rebels have reacted if McEnery had tried to sit on them? I bet they would have punched him in the stomach, pushed him away. I should have done that, but would it have really mattered? Who knew? And was it such a big deal? I survived. I hadn't been wounded or crushed. I tried to minimize the experience, to bargain it down to a fraction of itself. That helped a little, and then I asked myself if there was some strength I could salvage from the experience. My mind went blank.

Rather than getting into bed when I put my pajamas on, I left Tim half-asleep and went along the hall toward my parents' bedroom. With the night-lights on, the upstairs ceiling came to life with shadowy figures shaped by the lengthening table legs and the curving banister that wound around the landing. Maybe I didn't need to tell my parents what had happened. Maybe I could manage on my own. I debated the question with myself, standing outside their closed French doors. I didn't want to worry them, no matter how worried I was.

In spite of my misgivings I went into their room and flopped onto their bed. "Please don't make me go back tomorrow," I muttered to myself. "I'll do anything, but don't make me go back there tomorrow."

My father came in from the dressing room and saw my tears. "What's wrong, Jon?"

"I don't want to go back to Adams. I can't."

"Why?" he asked simply. He looked at me, giving me his full concentration. "What did they say to you?"

"They said I was too thin and needed to be stuffed." My mother came in from the bathroom and sat down with us on the bed.

"He doesn't want to go back to school," Dad said. "Look, there are a lot of things that we don't want to do, and we do them as best we can. It even happens to me. You have to go back. If you don't, you let them get the better of you. I'm not going to force you, but you have to go back. But what really happened?" For a second it felt like he was on my side, and that stopped the slide into further despair.

"Do I have to say? It's embarrassing. I don't want to." They allowed me not to answer, and I felt sad and brave that I had kept the secret to myself.

My mother told me to lie down on their bed and try to go to sleep. I closed my eyes but woke up a little while later and heard them whispering to each other. "Why did we send him to that school?" she said.

"It was a mistake," he said. "He's not ready for it. He's too young, too immature physically."

They saw I was awake, and my mother said, "You have to go back to Adams. We wouldn't know where else to send you. I don't even think the public school would take you at this point. It's time to go to sleep."

I walked back down the hall and didn't remember the next morning climbing the ladder to my upper bunk. Tim was wheezing slightly in the lower one, but I could tell he was sound asleep. When his asthma was bad his breathing had an erratic scraping rhythm. Those nights, each breath was more phlegmy and deeper than the last, and neither of us could sleep. This more gentle noise couldn't possibly keep either of us awake.

The next thing I knew Mom was shaking my forearm. The sun was already out. I slid down the ladder and put my clothes on. Tie and jacket last. I found my father, who was shaving in front of the mirror and so far hadn't nicked himself. "You're going to make it," he said when he saw me. "I don't know how exactly. But somehow."

A few minutes later Ole honked the school bus horn in the back driveway and I ran down the steps with a half-eaten corner of toast sticking out of my mouth.

# chapter 3

The next night at dinner the tone was more somber. Dad appeared preoccupied, even solemn. There were no number exercises or jokes. He was all business. Mom, sensing the change in him, drank an extra glass of white wine and nodded off briefly in her chair. Without saying, "You're in for it now," Tim looked at me sympathetically. Even Marianita was gloomy, her face downcast and dark, as if she knew there had been a shift in the house. I wished that Danny and Eileen were there to soften the mood.

"Jon, I have been thinking about you all day," my father said. "You have to bulk up, add muscle and weight, and I'm promising you that I will do whatever I can to support you. We're not going to let that school undermine you. That is my pledge to you." Usually he was satisfied with an overview of my situation and left the day-to-day details of managing my difficulties to Mom. But now his fervor in coming to my assistance transformed him. Was this how he stirred up his salesmen at the conventions he traveled to so frequently?

"I don't want my son treated this way by a bunch of goys," he said. This was an unusual reaction from him. It was rare for Dad to take offense at anti-Semitic insults, although he told us that he'd been called a "Jewboy" many times growing up. Prejudice didn't interest him much. He was always eager to move on, to find common ground.

"For starters, your mother and I think you should start drinking chocolate milkshakes every day. Two of them if you can. Do you think you can manage that?" he asked.

"It doesn't sound so bad. I like chocolate," I answered.

"Okay, I'll make your first one after dinner. Save a little room," he said. "We also have some doctors in mind to see if they have ideas for you. Your mother will start setting up appointments. And I want you to start doing calisthenics every morning before school. We're going to show these people."

After dinner we went into the kitchen and made me my first chocolate milkshake, as if he had been making them every day of his life. I rarely saw him there unless it was to flip pancakes on Sunday mornings. He watched me closely as I took the full glass in my hand. The first few frothy sips were enticing. The next ones were manageable if less exciting. When I put the glass down on the counter and saw how much was left, I realized what an effort it would take to finish it. With his eye on me, I forced myself to keep drinking. My stomach felt suddenly like it was going to burst. "Not sure I can do this every day," I said, avoiding looking at him.

"It'll be better if you drink it when you get home from school and it's not optional," he told me. Looking on the bright side, I thought that might help my after-school hunger, but the last mouthfuls looked as large as the mound of rice that rose from my plate at McEnery's lunch table. The smaller my gulps of the thick liquid were, the fuller the glass seemed. Finally, with just a thin covering on the bottom I put the glass down on the counter. I felt like I might be sick. "Great job!" my father said in a voice that sounded insincere and that he meant Mom to hear.

His interest in my body felt uncomfortable, like an invasion. McEnery had forced me to eat, and now my father, who I admired more than anyone for his savvy in the world, seemed to agree with him.

"Tomorrow I'm going to have a chin-up bar installed in your closet. Every time you go in I want you to give me ten pull-ups, all right? In the morning you can do push-ups and sit-ups. The same when you get back from school after the milkshake. How does that sound?" he asked.

I wasn't sure whether he was seeking a real answer or not, so I didn't look up from the bottom of the glass. This attention made me think that I had been assigned a personal drill sergeant who had a clear image of what my finished form should be. All I wanted was to have enough energy left to climb into my bunk bed, turn on my brown felt light, and read until I fell asleep. I had brought *The Hobbit* home from the Adams library, and it fascinated me. Muscles, weight, stature, and most sports didn't interest me at all compared with *The Hobbit*. I decided that I would pay lip service to his program and only pretend to participate.

The next morning he came into our bedroom and said, "Let's start with push-ups. Get down here." In a dream state, I slid down the bunk ladder and lay facedown on the orange rug. Tim was barely awake, with only one eye open. "Okay, ready? Start!" My first three push-ups showed conviction and vigor. The second three were less certain. The next three were painful. The last one was hopeless. He was all encouragement. "Some of the finest first push-ups I've seen. Next time try not to sag in the middle so much. Keep it fluid. Ten more?" I looked up at him in disbelief. This was beginning to feel like corporal punishment rather than bodybuilding, or maybe they were the same. I was already sick of it.

"Can I do them later?" I asked.

"Sure," he said. "Twenty sit-ups, then. Touch your elbow to the opposite knee. Go!" The same pattern ensued: initial gusto, intermediate hesitation followed by despair. I was unable to rise for the final five, which he counted off symbolically.

Many of my father's ideas of strength and virility came from his days in the air force training to be a pilot. He spoke with reverence of the discipline and physical demands that had been part of his training. When he was feeling expansive, he told his older sons about the calisthenics he did, exercise after exercise. For him and the other young men, exercise was also a form of punishment. If he hadn't made his bed correctly or his shoes weren't shiny enough, he had to do ten push-ups. This reminded me of the demerits I had had to run on the Adams hill. He was drawing on his air force experience to turn me into a man.

The chin-up bar was installed in the closet door frame the next day. That night when he got home, he did one chin-up for me, still dressed in his office suit and tie, to set an example. Only one, I thought to myself cynically; even I could do one perfectly. Ten was a different story. As before, I began with a now familiar surge of strength. In the mirror in front of me, I thought I could detect my torso lengthening and my arms thickening into heavy wire cables. The first four or five pull-ups I was thrilled by my power, but then I started to hang down longer and lower between each one before trying to pull myself back up. The bar felt higher above my head. I tried it with my palms facing in and facing out to see which was easier. Neither. By the ninth, I was a dangling sinew. The tenth I couldn't manage and dropped to the floor in a heap. I was already sore and angry at him. I never wanted to do another pull-up again.

"Not bad," he said. "Not bad at all. I don't think I could do ten either."

My father had never been an athlete. He went on an annual ski trip and took me with him on the occasional Sunday to his men's tennis game, which was more social than physical. While he played with his friends, I hit against the backboard for a few minutes or until all of the balls had sailed over the fence into the poison ivy. Then I'd sit down in one of the Adirondack-style lawn chairs and read until they were finished. It was hard to concentrate on the sentences hearing their curses in Yiddish and the whispers followed by laughter that I wasn't meant to understand. Occasionally, the men would look in my direction. I imagined that they were wondering why my father had brought me so I squinted back at them and then concentrated on my book as hard as I could. Was Dad telling them about the athletic regimen he'd designed for me? Just in case, I tried to sit as tall as I could in the uncomfortable green chair.

Mom, on the other hand, exercised briskly and regularly with the encouragement of Jack LaLanne's coaxing, chirpy voice on TV. Dad called these sessions "ladies' maintenance regimens." They were not really exercises that a man would do, or at least he wouldn't, if he did any. This condescension did not prevent him from having a discerning eye for ladies' workout clothing. "She looks fit," he'd say to us as an aside, winking, as we'd walk along the Chappaqua streets on the weekend. Or "Isn't she trim?" he'd ask Tim and me rhetorically.


When I watched my father shave, I examined him closely to see what the difference was between his torso and mine. He'd always told me that as a kid he had been just as scrawny as me. But by the time he was in his mid-forties and starting to look fleshy, it was hard for me to imagine what he'd looked like as a boy. As many times as he told me how thin he'd been, I refused to believe it. Did that mean that he had also been bullied at school and had kept it inside him like an internal sore that had never healed? Is that what he was trying to protect me from?

Over the next few months I was able to digest the chocolate shake without gagging and managed ten chin-ups at a time. I could work past the painful knots in my wrists and forearms and the daily fear that my muscles would never uncoil, but there seemed to be no appreciable increase in my weight. Every few days my parents would check the bathroom scale as if I were a boxer before a fight, but the needle barely moved past fifty pounds. They'd shake their heads in dismay over the situation. My father would repeat one of his favorite mantras: "With the eating comes the appetite," as if it would magically become true simply by him saying it.

The lack of progress discouraged me, too. It wasn't my idea to gain weight, but if I was making the effort and there was no change, what was the point? Maybe I could stop the exercises and just do what I preferred? When I suggested this to Dad, he gave me a look that said, Give up? How could we give up when we're just getting started? His disappointment made me want to renew my dedication to the program, to please him and graduate into the fuller life he envisioned for me.

And yet, I still doubted that I was as skinny as everyone believed I was. When I was alone in my bedroom, I would sit on the edge of my desk chair and unbutton my shirt. I would lean over my waistband, bending my chest toward my knees. Doubled forward, I grabbed the accumulated flesh around my stomach and pinched it into a wedge. The thick fold of skin was proof that the problem of my skinniness existed mostly in the minds of those around me.

On Sunday evening after my exercises Dad pulled me aside and told me that Mom had made a special appointment for me with Dr. Brewer, my orthodontist. "Maybe he can make an accurate prediction about your size so we can see what else needs doing."

"What do teeth have to do with it?" I asked.

"He claims he has instruments that measure the length of the dental roots and then he compares them to other bones. That's the theory at least. From that he can make a prediction. It sounds like bullshit to me, but your mother believes it," he said in an attempt to align us as men in a shared skepticism. That didn't disguise this being a higher level of intervention than his forcing me to eat and exercise. The heightened scrutiny made me feel vulnerable and nervous.

A few days later I drove with Mom into downtown Ossining, the nicer part that still had doctors' offices and movie theaters instead of deserted buildings and rubble. Dr. Brewer was a large, round man with curly hair barely covering his large head who always seemed to be on the verge of drooling. He narrated his procedures step by step without swallowing, and his saliva made a swishing noise. He had fitted me for braces a few months before, and I slept with my nighttime retainer on, the sheets hiding paths of miniature rubber bands in their folds.

"Sit down, Jonny. This won't hurt. I'm going to be taking a series of measurements, and with a few calculations I'll be able to make a fairly reliable prediction about your adult height and weight. Relax." He pulled a caliper out from his ribbed sky-blue dentist's tunic and started to measure my forearm. "Good. Now open your mouth wide." He slid some kind of ruler into the back of my mouth and held it there for a minute against my gum line. His face was so close to mine, I could hear the spit sloshing in his mouth. He wrote some figures down on a little pad that looked miniscule in his beefy hand. "Excellent. Excuse me for a moment. I need to throw these numbers into my charts, and I'll be back in a minute."

My mother came into the half-open stall where I was reclining, and I could see from her smile that good news awaited us. She took my hand in hers and gave it a little squeeze.

Dr. Brewer returned and said, "Well, I think you're going to like these results, Jean. According to my calculations, I predict that Jonny will be six foot two and weigh a hundred and sixty-five pounds when he reaches full adult size."

I smiled, and my mother beamed as if it were the happiest day of her life. In her own way, Mom wanted me to be tall and filled out, too. She was as invested as Dad was in my physical betterment. She worried about my ears sticking out and my overbite. She made appointments for me with plastic surgeons to see about pinning my ears back and checked that I wore my retainer every night. She even tested the rubber bands to make sure they had enough snap in them to perform their nocturnal function.

We thanked Dr. Brewer and floated home on a cushion of air. I pictured myself as a giant roaming the lunch hall at Adams bumping into the peons beneath me and barely noticing them as they bounced off me. My parents' pride in me would be immeasurable. The mark McEnery had made on me would be magically filled.

We announced the news to my father that night at dinner. While he nodded sympathetically at first, he turned to my mother, suddenly incredulous: "How can he know that? Does he just make it up? The man's a charlatan. Just in case he's wrong, eat more food. Jean, I think you should take him to see Dr. Diamond next week. If that doesn't work, I'm going to bring him to a specialist in the city."

Later that night he came into my room and asked me to do my usual routine of chin-ups. As he spoke, I straggled up the bar before plummeting back down. "I don't want to spoil the good news, but that guy has some imagination. He'll tell you whatever he thinks you want to hear. Let me tell you a story. Fifty or sixty years ago, after the First World war, there was a little boy who grew up in one of the richest homes in Europe. He could have anything he wanted whenever he wanted it. He only had one problem. He was unable to speak. Not a single word. He'd point to the food, or toys he wanted, and they would be handed to him. At first his parents weren't worried, but by the time he was six or seven they thought they better figure out what they could do for him. They took him to the greatest throat doctors, who had examined the opera singers of the day, but they couldn't find anything wrong with his vocal cords. After visiting doctor after doctor, they gave up and took him home. That Christmas they went to St. Moritz. His mother brought him skating one very cold afternoon. To warm the skaters up, hot chocolate was served. The boy took one sip and spat it out in disgust. 'Christ, that's hot! What are you trying to do to me?' His mother was beside herself with joy. 'You can talk! It's a miracle!' she said. 'Why didn't you speak until now?' The boy said without pausing: 'Because I never had to!'

"So the reason I'm telling you this, Jon, is that now you have to eat. You have to do this for yourself. If I eat for you, I'm the one who'll get fat. Now is the time for you to nourish yourself just in case your orthodontist and his wacky predictions are wrong. Do you follow what I'm saying?" he asked.

I nodded and dropped from the bar.


A week later Mom took me to Dr. Diamond, my pediatrician, whose office was in Chappaqua, on the ground floor of an old Victorian house where the floorboards squeaked. He was as interested in his patients' young minds as he was in their bodies and always asked what books we were reading and what we thought about them. His full head of dull white hair and the bright look in his blue eyes suggested he had an almost mystical wisdom to impart. My mother explained why we were there and Dr. Brewer's calculation. He listened and didn't say anything. He asked me to take my shirt off and felt the bones in my forearm carefully and knowingly, as if there might be deep meaning inside them. "Let's see what you weigh first," he said. I stepped on the scale and saw the silver marker just nudge past the fifty-pound mark. He looked at the records of my previous visit. "About the same as before, Jean. There is some science to support what your Dr. Brewer said. But not much." He paused and smiled. "So, Jon, how much would *you* like to weigh? How tall would *you* like to be?" he asked, as if I had a say in the matter.

The idea that I might have my own vision for what I wanted my weight to be had never occurred to me before. I didn't know what the right answer was or if there even was one. "Well, I guess, the same size as my parents. And one day I'd like to be over a hundred pounds," I mumbled, as if I were grasping for a number that would make them pleased with me. But as soon as I said the words "a hundred pounds," the shapes of the numbers lit up in my mind with a fluorescent satisfaction that announced something improbable, almost surreal, like the year 2000. I repeated it and it felt like it was almost mine even if it had been inspired by my wish to placate them. I wanted to weigh a hundred pounds. The assertion didn't fit me immediately but it felt like a vow that I could come to believe in. Just the images of the one followed by two zeroes made me proud of myself, although I didn't weigh an ounce more. Their approving looks confirmed that I had chosen well.

"That's a good answer, Jon," Dr. Diamond said. "You be what you're going to be. Stop worrying about him, Jean. He'll be fine." He looked at my mother reproachfully.

But after that burst of enthusiasm, my father's exercise program, the chocolate milkshakes, and the constant exhortations to eat just a little bit more, only two bites, how about three with an extra one for Grandma Ida, took their toll. Rather than making me feel that I was on the verge of a new, expansive future, the constant command to eat gave me the impression that I was falling further behind and my situation was deteriorating. This increased my doubts about the enterprise and made my father's vision for me seem unlikely, unachievable. I wanted to ask him why he wouldn't let me reach my natural weight by myself. Why did I have to try so hard to do something that I had only a passing interest in? Why did he need to impose it on me?

Many nights when I lay awake in bed on the top bunk thinking about these questions I imagined myself without a distinct body. I could feel my fingers and my toes, but I had no sense of my overall size. In the pitch blackness, I could stretch any part of my body at will. Or instead of being my usual shape, I could be no shape, a protoplasm, and this amorphous state felt better to me. It contained no basis for comparison, no hierarchy, no trace of mockery or intimidation. In this formlessness, my fears about myself became solvable and bearable. The darkness offered a refuge from criticism, and I lay awake reveling in it. Words from the end of "Fern Hill" drifted back to me: "green and dying", "sang in my chains."

After we went to bed, Tim's asthmatic wheeze mingled with other usual nighttime sounds. Suddenly afraid, I imagined that the sounds were no longer attributable to my brother, or the wind, or the trees but were actually the preparations of arsonists who were going to set fire to the house. Incapable of going back to sleep, I slipped out of my room and woke my mother up. She brought me into her dressing room so we wouldn't disturb Dad, who was a light, fitful sleeper. I stretched out on the settee with its curved wooden back. Sitting on the stool of her vanity, she faced me, her back to the mirror where she spent hours preparing for her dinner parties surrounded by her hairpieces on their Styrofoam skulls, her hairbrushes and necklaces, the little padded silk pouches of bracelets and rings, each in its given place. The crystal bottles of perfume were lined up on the glass tabletop in front of the mirror that covered the whole wall. Even in the dark, I knew where each item belonged. I had spent so much time with her there that my father, out of envy or spite, had taken me aside more than once to warn me, "If you spend too much time backstage, you'll lose interest in the performance. It's not healthy for a boy."

When she talked to me while she was getting herself ready, I had difficulty concentrating on what she said. I was so distracted by watching her train her hair strand by strand, intoxicated by the aroma of hairspray and perfume that swam together to create a unique scent, fascinated by how she mixed her bracelets and necklaces and rings. I couldn't believe how little time it took her to become beautiful.

"I thought I heard intruders talking outside the house. I don't know why, but I thought they were going to set it on fire. I can't get rid of the idea and can't get back to sleep," I said. She listened without interrupting me.

"Could you see them? Did you recognize any of them?" she asked in earnest.

"No, I could only hear their voices. The sounds weren't the ones I usually hear at night. Like fingernails scratching on the stucco or like matches being struck, and half-empty gasoline cans banging together."

"I think maybe you were dreaming about lighting the candles. Maybe you are turning the fire against yourself. There are no arsonists here, Jon." She reached for my hand and held it between her interlaced fingers. I could hear my father shuffling toward the dressing room in his robe and leather slippers.

"What's the matter?" he muttered.

"Jon thought he heard people outside. Would you go have a quick look, dear? Then we can all go back to sleep." Dutifully, he plodded downstairs. We could hear the front door open and shut and his tread on the carpeted stairs.

"I looked around, Jon, and even went out on the landing. There was no one there. I promise you. But also I want to say that although it is not impossible, the chances of someone coming to this house, this street, this town, are one in a million. Could it happen? Yes, theoretically, but it's as statistically likely as one of us being eaten by a bear in our own woods. Do the math yourself. There are no bears here."

"But we live so close to the highway. Someone could drive up, invade the house, attack us, and escape easily," I said.

"It's possible, but the odds are against it. Can you go back to sleep? Do you want me to sit with you for a while? Do you want a sleeping pill?" he asked. Mom had left us and gone back to bed.

"I think I'm all right, but Tim's wheezing. He's not awake yet, but it's pretty bad. I think he's going to wake up soon," I said, hoping he would come sit with us as he often did when Tim's asthma attack was severe.

"Has he had a Tedral yet?" he asked me.

"I don't think so. I didn't see him take one," I answered.

We paused at the door to listen to Tim. Each breath sank deeper into his lungs. His asthma had been diagnosed a year before, and Mom had taken him for a battery of tests. The skin on his arms and back was pricked with the spores of every local plant and fruit and leaf. I had lost track of all the things he was allergic to. It seemed to me the whole world was an irritant to him. While we stood there, he awakened and turned around toward us, sensing our presence.

"I'm glad you guys are here," Tim said. I climbed into my bunk, and Dad sat at the foot of his bed. My instinct was to distract him from his labored breathing. I liked Dad being there with us as if we were on the same team or at least all in the same bunkhouse. It almost felt as good as when he sat down and watched *Gilligan's Island* with us on a Saturday night when they didn't have a dinner party. We all laughed at Gilligan's ineptitude and the Skipper's paternal indulgence of him and irritation with him. There were no differences between us.

"Tomorrow, let's ride our bikes to the house in Millwood where the Nazi sympathizers used to meet. What was it called again?" I asked.

"How many Tedral have you had?" Dad asked.

"Two. I just took them," Tim answered.

"It was called the Bund Hall. Not much to see now. Just an ordinary house."

"Were there really Nazis in Millwood, Dad?" I asked, thinking about the noises that had bothered me until Tim's wheezing took my mind off them.

"Don't get carried away," Dad said, admonishing me. "It was called the Volksbund. They were local people from German backgrounds who met to talk things over. A bund is a club. They weren't really Nazis, but there were a few pro-Hitler nuts mixed in with the regulars."

The door opened, and Mom came in wearing her blue quilted robe. She went over to the blinds and pulled the curtain down after she straightened out the slats. Randomly, she moved around the room fussing over the treasures we had collected: rocks we thought were Indian arrowheads and glass shards that we imagined were pieces of colonial beer bottles. On her way out, she stopped near Tim and put her hand on his forehead.

"I hope you feel better tomorrow, dear," she said, and left.

Dad stayed, content to be with us no matter how long the asthma attack took to exhaust itself. Unlike his usually restless, active self, he was supremely calm during these vigils. During the lulls in conversation when the room was silent, Tim's wheezing made the noise our brooms made on the slate patio stones that Mom made us sweep again and again before we carried out the white wrought iron furniture each spring. Every time we thought we'd swept all of the catkins and acorns into the border grass she found another one and we had to start over again. It was like shoveling snow in a blizzard.

"All right, shh, guys," Dad said, even though we were quiet. I knew that even if Dad or I diverted Tim, his asthma attack wouldn't stop when we hoped it would. A queasiness filled my stomach, and I took a deep breath. Tim's health problems lay at the outer limit of my ability to help him as an older brother. Because Dad was there, I was discharged from my duties and went back to thinking about the invaders.

I reviewed my escape plan in the event of a surprise attack. As soon as I heard the first footstep on the front stairs, I would slide down the ladder from my bunk and creep silently into Eileen's room to not alert her to the danger. I'd slither out her bathroom door onto the terrace she shared with my parents. I'd hoist myself over the railing and shimmy down the drainpipe. Ignoring the weird shapes of shadows, I'd run down the big hill and alert the police at the station near the bottom of our road—not just a survivor but a savior. Thanks to my efforts, my siblings and my parents would be spared. I would be redeemed by my bravery. I felt heroic already. My resourcefulness would be recognized, and my weakness and size would be unimportant compared with my nerve and stealth.

# chapter 4

The Cadillac Fleetwood Brougham that took my father in and out of New York City each day offered more than transportation. The backseat was his sanctuary, where he could spend an uninterrupted hour alone. Occasionally, he paged through the *New York Times* and thumbed the stacks of business papers that he brought home each night. Mostly, they stayed unread inside his briefcase as he stared out the window and listened to Bach's Unaccompanied Cello Suites played by Janos Starker, his favorite music.

Being alone with him in his car, traveling into what I considered his city, was a rare privilege. Attilio, his giant Neapolitan driver, steered the car along the route my father had selected, his mournful clown's face with spiky black hair beaming into the backseat via the rearview mirror. Dad was very precise in his driving instructions to Attilio. "Always pump the brakes. Never stomp on them. Remember, they are as sensitive as you are," he said. It was difficult for me to imagine that someone as big as Attilio could be sensitive. His height and girth made him seem invulnerable. "Anticipate the turns, don't yank the wheel," my dad repeated frequently, for my sake as a future driver as well as Attilio's.

The car was also his lecture hall, his pulpit, and he was uncharacteristically serious when we were alone there. He handed down his opinions and advice in a straightforward way without anyone to modify them or contradict him. After Dad had heard the details of my visit with Dr. Diamond over a meal of blanquette de veau that no one liked, he told us that he had made an appointment for me to see an endocrinologist in Manhattan. This didn't mean that he didn't have faith in Dr. Diamond's opinion, but he wanted confirmation. "We're not going to put all our chips on that orthodontist of yours or Dr. Diamond. I want you to see Dr. Ensler for a full workup. Some friends told me that he has access to a special growth hormone. I think we ought to hear what he has to say, no?" he said, ending his comment with a question as he often did to be sure there was no possibility of a misunderstanding.

I had never heard of Dr. Ensler before and didn't care what he had to offer so long as the visit provided me the chance to explore the city and be alone with my father in the car.

"What does an endocrinologist do?" I asked him.

"Well, I don't know about other endocrinologists, but this hormone Ensler found might give you a few extra inches. You wouldn't turn that down, would you?"

"Of course not," I answered, not sure what I was risking.

"Not that it's going to turn you into a basketball player or anything," he said, and smirked. My parents had come to watch me play once on the Adams junior varsity basketball team, the lowest level there was in the upper school. I sat on the bench most of the time until the coach realized they were in the audience. Then he said, "Wells, your turn. Astonish me." I did my best, but the ball felt as heavy as a cannonball. I made one throw toward the net before he benched me. Afterward my mother said, "You tried very hard, Jon. Didn't you?"

"Yes, I did," I said, as assertively as possible, under the circumstances.

Dad said, "Good job. What a stupid sport!"

"How does the drug work? Do you have to take it every day?" I asked him now.

"I don't know, Jon. You need to get more information. I have heard good things about him. That's all I know." I imagined Ensler as a dark-faced voodoo practitioner putting needles in me and magically extending my spine by manipulating it with his bare hands. That would be the kind of doctor Dad would know.

To emphasize his view of me as too thin, too short and too impractical, Dad had started calling me his luftmentsch, the Yiddish word meaning a combination of man and air - a dreamer, a man with his head in the clouds.

"That is what you are, Jon," he said to me, as if it were proof of my condition. "A boy of the air. You are so light that your feet barely touch the ground. I'm not even sure you know what the ground is. Do you?" he asked, lowering his head a notch and looking up at me with his brown eyes, sympathetic but with a wry, skeptical twist. "The luftmensch wanders from place to place without leaving a footprint. That is what he did in the old days. He skimmed the surface of the earth as if he had no gravity, no idea what gravity was or why it was important to be part of the earth. He had no job, no shop. He told stories as he traveled from town to town passing gossip off as information."

Luftmentsch became my regular nickname. When my growth spurt began, my limbs were uncoordinated, as though they weren't completely under my control. I tripped in odd places where he couldn't see anything to trip over and he laughed at me. When I saw how big a laugh the gag got from him, I did it again but this time on purpose, like a vaudevillian honing his craft. He laughed and I laughed with him, not because it was funny but because I thought I was fooling him into thinking it had been an accident.

"So, are you willing to give Ensler a try?" he asked, bringing me back to the conversation.

"Yes, of course. What if I don't like him?" I asked.

"Let's worry about that later," he said. "Just don't forget to go to the appointment. Jo has the information," he said, referring to the secretary he shared with my uncle Paul.

As if it were a delicate plum, Attilio placed the car very gently into its spot in the garage of the Pan Am Building, and I set off on my own down the escalator to the main floor of Grand Central Terminal. My mother was going to take the train later and meet me at the doctor's office, but as I was about to turn thirteen, it was determined that in the meantime I was old enough to take a few hours to myself in the city, visiting bookshops and record stores. This, more than anything, made it worth the price of going to a doctor I had no interest in seeing.

I loved the light coming in through the huge windows that made the broad open space of Grand Central feel like the inside of a cathedral, the gold stars on the murky green ceiling shining just for me. I followed the halls to Lexington Avenue past the giant bays where the trains pulled in and disgorged their swarming passengers. On the street, I pushed through the crowds to Third Avenue and into Sam Goody's and immediately downstairs to the huge basement.

That day I was hunting for Simon and Garfunkel's album *Sounds of Silence*. I had heard the title song on the radio many times already; I could feel the darkness they sang about inside me and envied how they befriended and serenaded it. Just as badly I coveted *Red Rubber Ball* by the Cyrkle. How did they ever think of spelling *circle* like that?

After splurging my entire savings of ten dollars on the two albums, I walked west up to Forty-Seventh Street and across Fifth Avenue to the Gotham Book Mart. To get there meant dodging the Hasidic diamond barkers with their long black coats, yarmulkes, and ringlets. They swarmed around me trying to steer me toward their shops to buy a gold chain or a locket. They were insistent and disinterested in the obvious question of what a slight, nearly thirteen-year-old boy would do with an engagement ring. I accelerated past them until I could see the metal fish sign that hung outside the bookstore's front door declaring WISE MEN FISH HERE. The vestibule was cluttered with photographs of large groups of people, Gotham's luminaries. The one that stopped me showed Dylan Thomas, lounging on a rug, a blubbery man with a baby's face, engulfed by a throng of admirers.

Unlike record shopping, when I went into a bookstore I didn't know what I was searching for. My objective was not to locate a specific book but to absorb the atmosphere of the place itself, the rows of books that filled every inch of the walls and rose like cairns from the floor, organized according to a magical system known only to the staff. I tried not to be caught staring at the employees as they hunted for a title, finding it by a homing instinct that I wanted to acquire. I loitered as long as I could, pulling books and scanning random paragraphs while trying to eavesdrop on the clerks giving advice to other customers. Like mediums, the booksellers seemed to have an intuitive sense of what book each of them needed. I wanted that knowledge, wherever it came from, to be poured into me.

Finally, I chose *The Painted Bird* by Jerzy Kosinski because it was a book that Dad had recommended to me about a boy on his own who was in trouble. The flap copy described him wandering from town to town in Eastern Europe during World War II without a family. By comparison, my life felt safe and easy.

For a man who mostly read balance sheets, Dad loved short stories. He kept a copy of *The World's Greatest Short Stories* by his bed with its gray battered cover and took it away with him when he went on vacation. He loved the tales of O. Henry and Saki and Chesterton. Saki's "The Open Window" was his favorite. He'd recount the plot to us about the hunters who never returned from their hunting trip, the widow who left the window open for them in case they came back. It seemed that Dad was still as intrigued by the mystery as he'd been as a boy. Were those ghosts or living men who returned to Mrs. Sappleton's living room each night? Like the narrator, Mr. Framton Nuttel, Dad wasn't sure whether the reader or Mrs. Sappleton was more delusional when they reappeared.

On another recent car ride into the city with my father he had cocked his head slightly and said, "I've been watching you, and I think you're taking too long on each page. Are you reading every word?" he asked. I looked at him, surprised that reading didn't mean that each word counted.

"Is that wrong?" I asked.

"Well, not wrong exactly, but who has time for the little words. Do you really need *the, and, if,* or helper verbs? Does the tense really matter? Those won't give you the gist of it. They can be skipped, and you won't be missing much."

He examined me to make sure I was following him closely. "No articles, prepositions, or pronouns is my motto. They just get in the way and jumble up the sentence. You need to get to the meat as quickly as possible. It's like when I take you to a restaurant. Do I say eat the vegetables and potatoes first? No, I say, 'Eat what I'm paying for.' I'm paying for the meat. Ignore the vegetables. If you take all of those bitty words out, you'll reach the same conclusion.

I call it vertical reading. Horizontal is for scholars. You don't want to be a horizontalist, do you?" he asked, daring me to say yes.

I forced myself to leave the Gotham to go back to Dad's office on the forty-fifth floor of the Pan Am Building. When I walked in, I went from office to office to say hello and make pleasant conversation with his key executives as my father had instructed. "You can't treat them like they don't exist. I depend on these people even if you can't understand that," he had told me. As most of them had known me since I was a little boy, they asked about my school, my sports, or my studies. There was a sense of safety with them, a feeling that I was protected by most if not all of them. The only exception was Harry, the sales manager from the Bronx, who took a dim view of me. He'd see a book under my arm and yank it out. "What are you reading that for?" he'd ask. "Did you read *Exodus* yet? *Marjorie Morningstar*? *Atlas Shrugged*? Those are real books. What you're reading doesn't amount to shit. Those books won't do you any good." Then he'd walk away shaking his head, the diamond in his ring sparkling onto the ceiling.

Jo Sullivan, the secretary my father shared with his older brother, Paul, had been working with the two for many years. Because she typed out the weekly family letters my father circulated to both pairs of grandparents, she knew the minutiae of our daily lives. When I poked my head into her office to say hello, Jo smiled through the brown hair encroaching on her cheeks and stood up to greet me, her gold bracelets clinking on her bony wrists. "I have an appointment to see Dr. Ensler," I said.

"Yes, here's the address. Your father is in a meeting and asked me to give it to you," she said. "Good luck," she added, as if she knew exactly why I was headed there.

I walked to Dr. Ensler's with trepidation, my new book gripped tightly under my arm, finding my way through the secret passageways between buildings and the pocket parks open at both ends to the crosstown streets. I was like Marco Polo on his first visit to the city—discovering my own route. I walked through bank lobbies, atriums, and narrow aisles on the sides of buildings until

I reached his office on Forty-Ninth Street. My mother was waiting for me.

Having sat with me in many medical offices already, she could tell I was more nervous than usual. "You don't have to agree to anything today. All you have to do is hear what the doctor has to say. I have a feeling this is one of your father's wilder ideas," she said as she fussed over my hair with her fingers and picked an invisible piece of lint from my lapel. I showed her what I had bought, and she spent a few minutes glancing at *The Painted Bird* and skimming the liner notes on the Simon and Garfunkel album.

Dr. Ensler was a tall, thin man with dark eyes and a somber face. He looked as if no matter how much he shaved his sucked-in cheeks, they would still be haunted by a shadow lurking beneath his skin.

"So, what's on your mind, Mrs. Wells? Jonathan, nice to meet you," he said, extending his limp, bony fingers.

My mother went through the details of my height and weight before arriving at the inevitable question, "What can you do for him?" as if I were invisible. He looked at me, reached for my arm, and felt it carefully, as Dr. Diamond had done.

"There is a new growth hormone available that is extracted from the pituitary gland, called HGH for human growth hormone. Its use is still controversial except in extreme cases. It has shown some promise, and I have started to offer it to my patients."

"Without it, what do you think the prospects are for Jon's height and weight?" she asked.

"Maybe five seven or eight," he answered. He looked at me oddly and said, "He'll always be light."

"And with it—what then?" she asked.

"He might get an extra inch or two if he does it every day for a long time, but it takes dedication. He has to learn how to inject it himself, but the nurse can show him that."

Although I maintained a placid exterior, I was stunned. Had Dad known about the shots before he sent me, or had he calculated that it would be better if Ensler told me himself? I hated needles more than anything in the world. Even Dr. Diamond, the kindest doctor I had ever met, couldn't give me injections without causing me to panic. The prospect of giving them to myself was unthinkable. Why did Dad have to correct my body? How had it offended him?

After saying something noncommittal, Mom led me out of the office and we walked back to Grand Central Terminal together. I felt nauseous and scared and only wanted to listen to the sound of silence—Paul Simon's or my own, it didn't matter— as soon as I got home. "You don't have to do this, Jon. I think it's an outlandish idea that only your father could come up with," she said as we walked. "I won't let him force you, either."

"Hello darkness, my old friend" circulated inside my head as the train raced along the Hudson River, the light blinking through the trees and the dirty window. This HGH was a step too far. I began to resent the image of masculinity that my father was trying to impose on me. The milkshakes and exercises were bad enough, but giving myself shots was simply unimaginable.

At the Ossining station we took a taxi home. As we pulled through Nepawhin's gates I noticed a number of cars parked at the end of our driveway next to the former gatehouse, which my father rented to Dr. Skelton, dean of Briarcliff College, and his wife. Briarcliff, a short car ride away, was a women's college, and Dean Skelton, I suddenly remembered, hosted tea parties on his lawn for the graduating class twice a year.

When the taxi dropped us off in the front driveway, I bolted inside and up the stairs two at a time, bursting into our bedroom, where Tim lounged in his bunk. "Skelton is having a tea party. Come on. Let's move."

Soon we were crossing the gravel courtyard and heading down the stone steps between the box hedges on either side, past the yucca plants and the other exotic shrubs that Mom collected and scattered around the property. After touching the white stone lions' heads that guarded the rose garden for luck, we got down on our stomachs and crawled commando style across the grass. When we reached the hedge that separated our garden from Dean Skelton's, we burrowed under it like experts.

Close to the other side we could already hear the girls' voices volleying across the lawn. It felt as if we had come upon a flock of swans that had mysteriously landed on our property. They all sat the same way with their legs, in sheer stockings, glued together and tucked beneath them. They sipped tea with their pinkies in the air and with the other hand gestured to a friend on the other side of the lawn as if they were in a demure ballet. They wore twinsets and pearls and bright red lipstick, some of which stuck to the tips of their front teeth. We crept as near as we could, summoning all our adolescent stealth. We were so close, we could smell their perfume and could have reached out and touched them if we dared. In a state of complete fascination we watched them, barely remembering to breathe.

I wanted to get close to one of them, any one, to rest my head on her camel skirt or nest the back of my head on her wiry bra until I could make out the contours of her breasts while she leaned over me, to feel her humid breath on me and catch the little wavelets of her scent. She'd lay her light, bare arms across my rib cage and say anything she wanted to. I'd fidget, pretending to find her most comfortable place, until I had rubbed against every part of her I could.

Then the closest girl spotted us and elbowed the girl sitting next to her. "Look, we have some little puppy friends," she said. "You're not invisible, you know. We can see you under there." I felt the blood pool up in my face. Being caught was bad enough, but being called a puppy was worse. I was almost thirteen. Wasn't I almost a man?

"Why don't you come out and talk to us. It's nice to have some boys around, even if you're on the small side. How old are you boys?" she asked. "Let me guess. You must be eleven. You are so cute. Is that your younger brother, or is he older?"

"Younger," I said.

"How old is he? Ten?"

"We're both a lot older than you think," I bragged.

"Wouldn't you like to take them home and keep them in our rooms?" she said to her friend, and reached back with her palm to fluff up her heavy blond curls. "We could bring them little saucers of milk and feed them every night. They are so adorable. I want the older one, okay?"

Tim and I were frozen in our places under the hedge branches, unsure if we should creep forward or withdraw before they humiliated us further.

"Are you boys shy? Come out and talk to us. Is that your house?" she asked, pointing up the hill. We nodded. "And are you supposed to be down here now spying on coeds? Do your parents know you're here?" We shook our heads.

I looked at Tim as if to say, Let's get out of here before this gets worse. Then we crawled back from the hedges and took off at a gallop. We raced through the rose garden and up the stone steps. Within seconds we were inside and up the front stairs. When we reached the safety of our room, I slammed the door behind us as if to shut out the hordes of coeds who might be chasing us to tear us to pieces.

To calm us down I put Simon and Garfunkel on the turntable. "I am a rock … and a rock feels no pain" was our best hope at that moment. In addition to the humiliation, I thought it was unfair to Tim, who was bigger for his age than I was. Unlike me, he was a wrestler, and strong. He had a sturdier body and always weighed ten pounds more than I did.


At dinner that night Dad announced that he had spoken to Dr. Ensler after the appointment. Ensler thought I would make an excellent candidate for HGH therapy. "It's expensive, but what's money for if we can't protect our health and the health of our children?" he said grandly. I fidgeted in my chair, picking at the straw matting on the seat. "Are you ready to commit, Jon? We're in this together."

I looked first at the food that was left on my plate, then at my sister and brothers, and finally out the window, trying to find a place where my eyes could rest. I couldn't get a word out. I opened my mouth to say I couldn't do it, but no sound came out. An increasingly awkward silence filled the room.

"So what's wrong with you? If you don't think you can give your-self the shots, maybe Marianita could give them to you. She used to be a nurse in Ecuador, you know?"

"She was?" I asked, staring at my parents. Mom was impassive, not giving me a clue to whether this was a fact or a fabrication. "I didn't know that. Is that true?"

He looked away from me, trying to keep the absurdity of his claim to himself.

"That's what I was told, but it's unconfirmed. I have never seen the certificate," he said, improvising. I looked at my shoes, and then I heard him try to smother his laughter until he couldn't contain himself. He laughed so hard, his face turned red and he started to cough. It must have been the image of Marianita, who'd only seen a doctor once in her life, injecting me with growth serum that set him off. Perhaps it was her white uniform that sparked the idea of her being a nurse. When he laughed like that, it was hard for the rest of us not to join him. I thought, When the king laughs, everyone laughs with him. Even Mom, who seemed increasingly tired of his juvenile humor these days, smiled in spite of herself.

"Okay, I made it up. Can't a guy have some fun? Do you want to do it or not, Jon?"

"I don't think I can give myself the shots. I just can't."

"All right. Fine. I'm not going to force you. We'll have to find another way to make you want to grow up. Let's just drop it."

One weekend, a few days later, Tim was away on an overnight school trip and I decided to sleep in his bottom bunk. When I awak-ened the next morning, my eyes focused on the cover of the *The Painted Bird*, which I had wedged into the slats of the top bunk. The bird with its brightly colored feathers peered down at me from the cover, its sharp face glaring from its mantle as if it were one of the alluring females who had been flirting with me on the lawn.

I didn't know whether I had been dreaming about the coeds at Dr. Skelton's house before I woke up or just imagined them again when I began to notice how aroused I was. I pictured the two girls who had spoken to us rotating and exchanging places with each other. The more I watched them moving and coming back to life, the more excited I became. This wasn't the first time those Briarcliff College girls had affected me. Absentmindedly, I touched myself through the sheet. I closed my eyes, and a kaleidoscope of their clothes and stockings and pearls, their hairdos and scents and crimson lipstick, even the smudge marks on the white Kleenex they used to remove the stain from their front teeth, overwhelmed me. I searched my memory to remember tiny details of their features in order to complete them and preserve them. They leaned forward to ask me another question, twisting over their hips toward me. Their white hands floated up and gestured across the lawn, then rested in their laps, where I wanted to land most of all.

Suddenly my bedroom door creaked open. I didn't have enough time to hide myself or turn around to see who it was before Mom entered, circling behind my head and settling at the foot of the bed. I tried to disguise my actions, to be uncaught. It didn't occur to her to pause, to notice the motion, and leave me in privacy. She walked in as if my room were hers and she had every right to be there.

"Is that a wee wee erection?" she asked, fixing me in her eyes and not blinking. I had no idea what she meant. Erections of any kind were new to me. She waited expectantly for my answer. Her blue eyes twinkled, and she had a benevolent, patient cast to her face.

"You know I didn't have any brothers growing up, so I never learned these things. I heard some boys get those in the morning when they haven't gone to the bathroom yet. Is that what yours is?" she asked, as if we were siblings.

"Or is it the other kind?" I didn't know what to say. I couldn't bear to look at her. All the color faded from the room. It was black and white. The little light that came through the blinds was so dazzling that it was hard to see. The rest of the space was like dusk, although it was the beginning of the day. Suddenly, I felt naked, as if a prankster had stolen all of my clothes while I was sleeping. I searched my brain for camouflage, anything that would cover me.

"I think I need to go back to sleep," I managed to say. I turned away from her, more mortified than if she had seen me undressed. How could I ever get the idea of her intrusion out of my head? The orange wall was two inches from my face, and I stared hard at it, hoping it would come into focus. In seconds I had been demoted from being her trusted eldest son and confidant to being one of the slobs she was on guard against: the uncouth ones, the leering ones, the slovenly ones who had dirt packed under their fingernails and whose shirttails hung out. In an instant I had become a fallible mortal. The opening lines of my favorite Beatles song, "You've Got to Hide Your Love Away," flooded in on me. I held my head in my hand and rolled onto my side to face the wall. I sang the chorus to myself as she left without another word. A heated-up, smoldering sensation inside me twisted and burned. I could feel the heaviness of John Lennon's shame and isolation. We were brothers in humiliation.

# chapter 5

B ecause my family was not observant, I knew I wouldn't have a bar mitzvah when I turned thirteen. Instead Mom baked a dark chocolate cake with milk chocolate icing. Thirteen candles in a circle were the symbol of my official arrival into manhood. I was seated in my father's chair at the head of the table. He was on my right, separated from me by a small clump of presents. Larger boxes formed a pile on the floor. After I cut the cake and had as big a slice as I could imagine eating, I put my fork down and paused before opening the gifts. The moment felt like a celebration that would stay with me and to which I could return for nourishment when I needed it.

As I unwrapped the presents, I didn't immediately grasp the pattern. There were books about London and Paris as well as *Collected Poems of Dylan Thomas*, which my mother had chosen for me—a gift from her alone. My maternal grandparents gave me a silver dollar and a polished shoehorn made from a moose antler. Then I turned to the big presents on the floor beside me. In each box was a blue tweed Brooks Brothers suitcase of a different size with a tan leather handle and my initials monogrammed on the top. When I opened the smallest one there was a Pan Am ticket for a flight to Geneva, Paris, and London with my parents at the end of the school year. I turned to them, my mouth open, speechless.

The intervening months passed uneventfully. Aside from my daily Latin class, McEnery ignored me and I avoided him. Before I knew it I was checked in and seated on the plane. I looked at my passport. It said I was four feet nine inches and weighed sixty-seven pounds. At that moment I didn't care about my size or my maturity. I had my own blue Pan Am flight bag with the longitudinal lines of the globe inked in white on a sky-blue background. The stewardess, with her radiant blond hair swept up into a little sky-blue cap, treated me like the special young traveler, an adventurer on his first flight alone across the ocean. I fell asleep forming in my mind a list of the sights from the guidebook that I wanted to visit the most. My parents, who had preceded me by a few days, met me at customs.

Our first stop was Lausanne, Switzerland, where my mother's closest friend from New York and her husband, Ellen and Nathan Mitnick, had moved a few years before so he could be closer to his business. Nathan was an obsessive art collector, and their house was filled with treasures. My first impression when I walked into the marble hallway was that I had entered a museum. Mom had warned me in the car that no piece of art was to be approached too closely, let alone touched.

"Admire at a distance," Nathan said, issuing the warning in his heavy northern European accent that my parents had informed me was German as we took off our raincoats. I was careful as we were led from room to room, but when no one was looking I let my fingers brush against the buxom curves of the life-size Maillol nude that stood at the top of the marble stairs. I noticed that her buttocks were more golden than the rest of her body, suggesting that my hands were not the first ones to caress her there. From the deck surrounding the pool, I looked out at the lake far below the hillside. Lake Geneva was a vast blue sea stretching all of the way from Geneva in the west to Montreux in the east and then leading to the foothills of the Alps. Across the lake in France, the white peaks poked through the clouds.

Nathan was a self-made man who sold classical music collections through the mail, hiring obscure orchestras to play the classic symphonies for albums that he sold to every home aspiring to high culture. He was as tireless in his marketing as he was in his art collecting. His lewd jokes of which he seemed to know an endless number were delivered in a lurid, guttural voice that disguised his seriousness and smarts. He was a tall man, very large around the waist. He beckoned to me, calling me Jonny, as if he had some old-world wisdom to impart. "Wouldn't you like to live with us for a little while over here?" he asked me. Since Nathan never said a word to me unless it was some kind of warning or rebuke, his offer was difficult to grasp. Was he lonely? Did he want me as a younger brother for their son, Eric, who only had an older sister?

Ellen Mitnick, who had grown up in Beverly Hills, was my mother's closest friend and former roommate in Manhattan after college. Their single lives were made up of boyfriends and dates, jobs that came and went, and adventures on the weekend. When the two women selected and married their husbands, both businessmen on the make, the men discovered they had similar work ambitions. Their competitiveness with each other, however, meant that they were never friends. My mother had often told me that Nathan characterized my father as "pushy," although I wasn't sure what that really meant. For his part, Dad confided to me that Nathan was so "swift" that he could "take off your socks without removing your shoes," a warning that kept me on high alert.

Eric was a few years older than I was and attended a local private school called École Nouvelle. Whenever we had been thrown together in the past at events organized by our mothers he looked down on me as if I had a bad smell that only he could detect. His animosity was strong enough to make me want to avoid him. When they visited us on the occasional Saturday, driving to Millwood from their apartment in New York City, and there was no escaping him, I could sense his barely contained anger. I never knew why it was directed at me or why there was so much of it.

The day we visited them Eric was away on a school trip, and this gave Ellen the chance to boast about his school. The few times I had overheard Ellen and Eric speaking to each other he had a mocking, surly tone. With me, she had always been indulgent. She liked to call me Jonny, a nickname I hated because it reminded me of the greasers in *West Side Story*, but that didn't make me not like her. She had curly red hair, freckles, and a sly smile that she tried to control but couldn't.

In Lausanne I heard a mixture of languages and accents that suggested exotic locations and stories of intrigue. I tasted food that I loved instantly and saw sights I had only seen in my parents' slides. In Paris we visited Sacré-Coeur and were stunned by its seamless whiteness. They took me to the Orangerie Museum, where I stared at the beauty of Monet's eight large *Water Lilies* murals in their round room. In London I bought *Between the Buttons,* the Rolling Stones' newest album, which I knew none of my school friends would have yet. My mother took me to shops on Carnaby Street featuring wildly flowered shirts and bell-bottom pants. I was converted to what I thought were European styles and never wanted to go back to America.

In addition to these revelations of the wider world, I had my parents to myself. They were on their best behavior sharing my excitement at the newness of my experience. I was the eldest son and was rewarded for it. During those two weeks all discussion of my size and weight was suspended as I tried new foods and basked in their attention. They showed me their best married selves. The opposition that I usually felt between them, each trying to convince me that the other's view of the world was flawed, was relaxed. In the absence of that tension, I didn't feel split between them as if I were their referee and had to declare one of them the winner. My father kept his wandering eyes and hands and stray comments about other women to himself and doted on my mother. She, in turn, didn't need to retaliate for his distractions because there weren't any. This made it easier for her to remember why she had married him. He was resourceful and energetic, spending his time with maps and schedules plotting our next excursion. When the conversation turned serious, he listened earnestly and thought-fully.

The prospect of this broader world inspired me to study French with much more gusto when I returned to school. Back home, Mom and Marianita figured out how to make the béarnaise sauce that I had fallen in love with and wanted to slather on everything. And yet, none of this affected my body. It wasn't long after our return that Dad started in on my problems again, as if we had never had a vacation from them.


Almost a year later and a month after my fourteenth birthday during one of my car rides alone with him from the city, he said: "So, when are you going to get back to work on your muscles? You know girls like something to hold on to. Only the weirdos want a scarecrow or a skeleton. That reminds me. I've been meaning to ask you, do you have a girlfriend yet?" I looked at him not sure if the truth was the right answer.

"I go to dancing school, if that's what you mean?" I answered.

"No, I know you go to dancing school. What I meant was, of the girls you dance with, is one of them special?" He had a facial tic, half shutting his left eye while scrunching up his left cheek, and as he looked at me now it was pronounced. Because his questions and mannerisms were so familiar, I missed how prying they were. He appeared to be genuinely curious, in a benign way.

"No, not really. I don't have a favorite, if that's what you mean. I don't really care who I dance with except for some of the tall girls. I avoid them."

"By the time I was thirteen, I had already had many girlfriends, but I lived in a city and there were lots of girls to play with. What kind of girl do you like?" he asked, getting a little impatient with me.

"I don't know yet, Dad," I said.

"You should start to think about it. You have no idea how exciting life can be with them," he said, and looked at me cryptically, as if he were speaking in a code I was only meant to understand in general terms.

"I can't imagine why they'd want to talk to me."

"Nonsense," he said. "They want you to talk to them, to transport them somewhere far away. Anywhere you'd like to go. Do you know what I mean?"

"No," I said.

"Well, you need to feed their imagination with a place they've never seen before, an unknown place. Describe it to them and take them there with your words. You have good words. Use them. Help them imagine it. Doesn't matter whether you've been there or not. They haven't been there either."

I recalled the standard question he asked young women we met on our hiking vacations. "Are you from Tacoma by any chance?"

Tim and I thought he must have some sixth geographical sense of knowing where a woman was from until we realized that he asked all of them the same question. He thought it was unlikely that anyone we met in the Northeast was actually from Tacoma or even knew anything about it. Once he was certain, he would begin to describe what a beautiful place it was, how the sailboats looked in the light on Commencement Bay, the arrangement of the islands in the distance, and the vague smell of cherry blossoms in the spring.

Whenever we heard Dad launch into his Tacoma gambit, Tim and I felt embarrassed but unsure who we were more embarrassed for, the poor girl or him. As he ran through his routine, throwing in new imaginary details, gesticulating to flesh out the scene, we looked at each other and rolled our eyes. Was the girl really interested or just being polite? we wondered. We couldn't believe anyone would fall for his yarn, so we distanced ourselves from him and avoided his dragging us into the story to be his witnesses or chorus. We slowed our pace and dropped farther and farther behind.

"So, why don't you have a girlfriend yet? Is there something you need to tell me?" he asked in his most sincere, nonjudgmental voice, which didn't sound like him. "If you were bigger and stronger, you wouldn't feel so uncomfortable with girls, or is that the problem?" He watched me closely to see if I would betray any hesitation when I answered him.

"I don't think that's the problem, Dad."

"Are you sure? Some men are just queer, you know. They can't help it. It happened to me once on a train to Albuquerque. I woke up in the middle of the night and some guy had his hand in my pants. I ran out of that compartment as fast as Jesse Owens. It happens. Is that who you are?" he asked.

My father had brought the "queer" question up to me before, when one of the Adams masters who oversaw a dormitory had been fired from the school for fondling a boy who lived on his corridor. I hadn't been as shocked by Dad mentioning this to me as I had been when I first heard about it at school. I was sorry for the boy, who reminded me of myself when McEnery was sitting on top of me. The feeling of exhaustion returned in its entirety. Was that how that other boy felt, weighted down by his master's act, coerced, unable to confess until someone caught them?

"No, I'm just nervous around girls," I answered.

"I'm not so sure you're giving me the whole story about girls versus boys, but there's one way to find out. I have a friend in New York who told me about a woman. Her specialty is young boys. I think you should meet her. If you don't go for her, I don't know what I can do to help you," he said. "He told me she was a beauty too, and gentle and kind and all that stuff women are better at than we are. What do you think?"

I could sense the intense concentration in his face. It was as if his olive skin turned a shade darker. His eyes narrowed, his patience faded, and he could only focus on me. His questions took on an urgency that he could not let go of. The outside world disappeared. I could tell though that this wasn't really about my size and weight anymore. This was about whether I preferred men or women.

I asked him who she was. He looked at me with his blank face, which I had seen many times before. It was the face that said: I know the answer, but I will never tell you. Often it appeared with a wink, but not today. Instead, he turned quiet and coy.

"New York is a vast city," he said. "There are treatments of all sorts for all sorts of problems." He added to this vague statement that it was traditional in Europe and other more ancient civilizations to initiate boys in this way. I knew he was lying or making it up because he gestured wildly when he said it, which was something he never did when he was telling the truth. He embellished this by adding that he felt it was his obligation to do this for me, his responsibility as a father.

At first I felt tantalized by his offer, excited, curious, tempted, but then it frightened me and I recoiled from it. What would he tell her about me? How would he describe my body? Would he mention my weight? Would he make the derogatory comments to her that he had made so often to me? If he did, and without knowing whether he had or hadn't, how could I not feel weak going to a strange woman's apartment and taking off my clothes?

I imagined her as one of Dr. Skelton's coeds coming to life. She wore a camel-colored skirt and a white blouse with the sleeves folded over showing her slender wrists and forearms. Everything about her was flawless. She walked toward me as if she were emerging from the landscape. She was real. She would be kind. There wouldn't be difficult questions to answer about my body. She would be tolerant of my inexperience. I would not be self-conscious about how skinny I was.

I examined Dad's proposal from a different light. If Dad's attention to other women was a violation of Mom's sense of propriety, it appeared to be his major hobby outside work. Perhaps I should consider his point of view, I reasoned, before dismissing it automatically just because it was his. It couldn't make me more uncomfortable than I was with her painful questions.

After he made his proposition, Dad remained silent. He seemed to be thinking through what he had offered, as though he hadn't known in advance what it was, examining it from different angles to see if there was a hole in it. As Attilio turned off the highway five minutes from our driveway, Dad said, "There's just one condition."

"What's that?" I asked him.

"Whatever you say or do, you must never tell your mother about this, *verstandt?*" he added, substituting Yiddish to emphasize the supreme importance of this condition. He stared at me without blinking. He was very aware of how much I confided in her and how often she confided in me. I knew too how jealous he was of my intimacy with her, and his proposition appeared to me a desperate attempt to create an event that would bond us in secrecy and subterfuge forever.

"This sort of thing is not something to be discussed with any women, especially your mother, not that there is anything wrong with it. Do you understand that?" He looked at me again, intently trying to convince himself that he could trust me. "I have never met this lady, but she comes highly recommended. Understood?"

"Yes." I nodded. "Do you know anything about her at all?"

"The only thing I can tell you is that she's Swedish," he said.

Although it wasn't much, this crumb of information was vital. During the previous year we had had a Swedish au pair living in our house named Gunilla. She was a big country girl in her early twenties who had never been to America before and missed her family. She was at least five feet nine, full-figured, and she wore her shining blond hair in a bun like Catherine Deneuve. She spoke English in a singsong voice, often putting the words in the wrong order. As if this were not already too overwhelming for Tim and me, she wore silver lipstick, which she always kept fresh and glistening: an au pair goddess we would follow anywhere.

Between my father, my brother, and me, there was a discreet competition for her attention. My father was cagey, not speaking with her much but letting her know with his dark sidelong glances how interested he was in her. Tim simply tried to find the shortest path to her lap. I wooed her by playing pop hits for her on my portable record player, from Petula Clark to Simon and Garfunkel to Tommy James and the Shondells.

When Gunilla explained the rituals of her cherished Santa Lucia festival, Swedish Christmas, we vied for the right to spend the evening in her room sitting as close to her as possible, asking as many questions as we could dream up about how her small town celebrated the occasion. Each of us wanted to be the one nearest to her, to inhale her scent and be brushed by her bare arms. Each of us wanted to be selected.

Gunilla was determined to make us Swedish, if only for Christmas Eve, a night we spent adding ornaments to the tree instead of celebrating. We sat on the carpet in her room while she cut up white sheets and fitted them over us. She explained that we were supposed to wear these costumes in the evening procession, as if we were visiting angels. We wrapped our measly presents for our parents in white tissue paper and sprinkled them with gold and silver stars. She covered her throw pillows in white to carry them on into our parents' bedroom. Around our heads we wore gilded laurels and sang the

Swedish songs that she had been making us listen to for weeks. My sister, Eileen, carried a plate of cookies called pfeffernuss.

This was almost all I knew about Sweden when my father passed along the only detail he was willing to share about my seducer. When I tried to imagine her before we met, I envisioned a physically reduced Gunilla, more comparable to my size and weight. She'd wear a short white corduroy skirt and offer me lemonade and maybe a cookie. She would be interested in only me. Her touch would magically transform me into a full-grown man.

A few days passed without Dad mentioning it again. One night he took me aside after dinner and said, "I hope you're not busy tomorrow? I'd like you to come to my office in the afternoon." I looked at him, asking myself the question I couldn't ask out loud. Was this the day?

The next morning I took the train into the city. I met my father in his office as he had requested after my usual stops at the book and record stores. I knocked on his door, and he let me in without making me wait outside. He said he had a quick call, so I sat down on the sofa and looked at the familiar paintings and carvings on the wall. I wondered how a few hours might change my understanding of them.

He continued his conversation from his table while I sat behind his black leather desk in his black leather chair, as if by sitting there I would have his authority conferred on me. I looked at the small brass plaque that he had kept on his desk for as long as I'd been visiting. It said, IF YOU CAN'T DAZZLE THEM WITH KNOWLEDGE, BAFFLE THEM WITH BULLSHIT. It faced out so every visitor could read it.

His call went on and I was getting bored, so I opened the desk drawer and rummaged through his assortment of foreign coins, miniature bars of Hilton soap, ponies of vodka, and his gag collection. This included a Styrofoam contraceptive device that the user was instructed to put between her knees and hold in place there. The information on the back of the package offered a refund in the event of pregnancy.

He hung up the phone and sat down opposite me. In his nearly illegible handwriting he scrawled the name Ingrid and her address, and pushed the scrap of paper to me across his desk..

"Throw the piece of paper away as soon as you leave, Jon. Leave no trace," he said.

Dad stood up and asked me to come with him, so I followed him into Jo's office. Jo's nimbleness with the brothers' secrets guaranteed her lifetime employment. Furthermore, she was able to keep them straight without committing them to paper. He went into a small cabinet and blocked what he was doing with his body. Burrowing there, he told me to go back to his office.

When he returned, he handed me an envelope that I instinctively held up to the light. Through the glue and the folds I could see there was a hundred-dollar bill inside. That seemed like an enormous sum to me. I dreamt of the books and records I could buy with it. As I was leaving, he said, "When you meet Ingrid, hand this envelope to her and then put it out of your mind. Remember, you are not inconveniencing her. You don't have to make excuses for taking up her time. Don't apologize, for Christ's sake. This is what she loves to do, so don't be shy."

In the taxi going uptown I felt oddly calm and sure of myself in an altered way, as if this were a natural step in my progression—from exercises to doctors to prostitutes. I floated in a sort of trance. On Madison Avenue the reddish tint of the sun on the brick buildings matched the burnt orange of the dresses in the shop windows. In the early summer the stores were filled with bright-colored clothes in busy, swirling patterns.

As I gazed at the pedestrians on the sidewalks, it seemed to me that their feet never touched the ground. Their legs moved languidly and without apparent effort. It was as if they were all underwater walking in slow motion. My brain detached from my body. I wasn't sure what I was feeling. My limbs were heavy. I was being commanded by someone via remote control. I was obedient yet skeptical. This wasn't really happening to me.

Ingrid lived on Madison Avenue and Sixty-Eighth Street. I got out on the corner. The Halston boutique was across the street next to a fancy shoe store that displayed a line of ornately winged gladiator sandals whose straps wrapped around the wearer's ankles and up the calf. Since I was early, I stared into the windows and wondered what magical female creatures would actually buy and wear them and if their feet would even touch the ground. I was not aware of any feeling, not even the desire I had felt for the coeds. I was weightless, as if gravity had released me.

When the exact time came, I walked down Ingrid's block and rang the bell. She buzzed me in, and I walked up two flights of stairs floor to her apartment and knocked. She opened the door, hiding herself behind it, and gestured me inside. She closed the door and pointed me to the sofa. I handed her the envelope, and she put it on the side table without opening it. She looked me over and smiled. She hung my raincoat in the drab closet.

My first reaction on seeing her was that she was an impostor. She had black hair, and I knew that this was impossible, as all Swedish men and women were blond. Not just because Gunilla was but so were Swedes in the movies and magazines. Was she pretending to be Swedish? Was she wearing a wig?

She asked if I wanted something to drink. While she was getting me a glass of water, I fixated on my surroundings. The room was small, and the walls were covered in a kind of nondescript indoor stucco that looked as if it might draw blood if I rubbed against it the wrong way. Beyond where we were sitting, there wasn't much furniture and there were no personal effects. Where were her family photographs? Where was the miniature Swedish flag and books and records like the ones Gunilla kept in her room? I scanned the empty counters and shelves. There was a courtyard window that had almost no light coming through, as if it were underground. Who or how could she live in a place like this? Or maybe this wasn't her place, I thought. But then whose was it?

When she came back and the shock of her hair color had worn off slightly, I was able to look at her more carefully without being caught staring. She was wearing a yellow top and pants that revealed a bare tan midriff. Through her dark hair she had tied a yellow scarf. She looked like she could be a friend of Annette Funicello or Mary Ann, the wholesome student shipwrecked on *Gilligan's Island*. I wanted to ask her a million questions but stopped myself. An otherworldly calm came over me.

"What's your favorite sport?" she asked.

"Skiing," I said, and racked my brain to think of any other sport. I couldn't remember why I liked skiing except we had always done it. Nothing else came to mind. My mind was blank. I hadn't come prepared to have a conversation. Nor had I imagined her sitting so close to me or her yellow scarf or the way her skin smelled. She took my hand and started tracing her dark red fingernail up and down my fingers. She moved closer to my right side and kissed me on the cheek. I shuddered, not sure if I was scared or excited or both.

"Such a pretty boy," she said. "How old are you?"

"Fourteen," I said. She seemed surprised.

"You are so mature for your age," she said, very close to my ear. She helped me wriggle out of my jacket, unbuttoned my shirt and peeked at my chest, then lifted the fabric so she could see the prominence of my ribs, the concavity of my stomach. I felt embarrassed when her fingers brushed over my abdomen, the epicenter of my thinness. Then she looked up at me again and smiled as if I had somehow, in some way that I could not possibly understand, made her day.

She put her hand flat against my chest and moved it along my shoulder before taking my hand. She stood up and led me to the next room and the mattress, which rested on the floor. Kneeling, she unlaced my shoes and put them neatly against the wall. She nested my socks inside, unbuckled my belt, and slithered my pants down my legs. I leaned my head back on the pillow and tried to focus on the tin pattern in the ceiling. I could see from the corner of my eyes how she took all her clothes off, except for her yellow scarf, as if we had known each other our whole lives. They rested on the floor in a little heap. Already, I could feel the warmth radiating toward me and I was entranced by how human she was—her scent and movement, how her dark hair sparkled. She was not a figment of my imagination.

When she lay down on her side next to me, she took my penis in her hand and moved it back and forth. After I had an erection, she lowered her head across my stomach and took it in her mouth. The feeling was intense and remote at the same time. I concentrated on the yellow scarf as her head made a figure eight pattern up and down and in circles. I could see the tips of my toes above her hair. She stopped suddenly and looked back at me and smiled again as if she had done something amazing for me that I should be grateful for. I smiled back, at a loss for words, and waited for what would happen next. I tried to avoid her eyes.

She guided my body on top of her and put me inside her. I moved in and out quickly. Her hands on my hips tried to slow me down. I felt broad and heavy between her thighs and knees, which squeezed me. Within a minute I stopped moving. She said nothing.

I lay inert on top of her. I felt that there was something I should say, but my words were stuck, as if my brain and tongue had stopped communicating. Possible phrases appeared. I loved how I felt inside her. I loved how her skin felt on mine, but that seemed too dumb and obvious to mention. I thought she was pretty, but surely she knew that already or she would have chosen a different profession. Guided by her hands, I rolled off and lay next to her. I wondered what she was thinking about but didn't say. What were her secrets? Did she have a child? A husband in Sweden? Another country? How many other boys had she known like me, I wanted to ask, but I sensed that such a question was off-limits no matter how badly I wanted to know the answer. Our arms touched, but the warmth felt thin.

She glanced at me and smiled. She didn't seem to think there was any need for words at that moment. I wanted to put my fingers in her hair to see how black hair felt but I didn't know whether I had permission to touch it once we were officially finished.

Unasked, I looked for my clothes and put them on slowly. I could feel her eyes on my back from the bed. She asked me if I would visit her again. Of course, I said reflexively. When I was finished getting dressed, she got up naked from the bed and put her arm around my waist and pulled me toward her. As she kissed me on the cheek

I could smell the mix of baby powder and perfume on her skin. I barely remembered my raincoat in the front closet.

"Please come see me again," she whispered a little more insistently in my ear. I heard the door close behind me and walked down the stairs, my shoulder rubbing against the wall for support, my hand on the dark banister. I looked at my watch. The session had taken less than an hour. I left her building and walked back downtown. I wanted to feel the pavement under my feet. I felt lonely against the fading sunlight, as if something enormous had happened that was also flat and hollow. I knew that I was supposed to feel triumphant, but it seemed as though my body had been fleeced.

On the car ride home Dad was especially quiet. He shuffled his business papers, closed his eyes, and listened to the classical music that was playing on WQXR, the radio station of the *New York Times*, as a grave voice announced every half hour. I knew his apparent disinterest was a feint. He wanted to hear every detail of my encounter but knew instinctively that he should let some time pass. When he couldn't wait any longer, he asked me a few banal questions as if I had gone to see a doctor with exotic medical symptoms whose tests might reveal a hidden illness. I gave him monosyllabic answers, suddenly determined to defy his curiosity.

I felt disoriented. I wanted to be by myself even if it meant leaping out of the car. I fidgeted with the electric windows like I was a six-year-old again, letting in a ribbon of cool air before closing it quickly. My hand grasped the door handle as if I were daring myself to yank it. I pictured myself jumping out while we waited at a stop sign. I would wander for a few miles before finally walking home. Was my body still mine, or had I just given it away? My hands could recognize the familiar bumpiness in my wrist bones and my ribs sticking out curved around me, but I wasn't sure how much of my body was still mine or whether I had ceded it to others. I badly wanted it back, so it would be mine again and mine alone.

# chapter 6

In the dark that night the chorus to the Band's song "The Weight" wove through my thoughts. I could feel the load being placed "right on me." I imagined its form. At first it took the shape of a big black dumbbell like the one Popeye couldn't budge in the cartoons, but I pressed to see it more clearly. McEnery's huge body flickered in space as if it were spinning free of gravity. Ingrid propped her left forearm on my torso. A resistance started to grow in me like a counterweight to them. But it wasn't heavy. The more I opposed Ingrid and McEnery in my mind, the more resilient I became. Something was hiding in me that made me stronger. It grew and I could feel it expand, a resilience that I alone noticed.

At dinner the next night the evening ritual was the same as it always was. We took our napkins out of the napkin rings and unfolded them in our laps. We made small talk waiting for the surprise that would be the evening meal. I struggled to convince myself that nothing had changed, that there had been no Ingrid, no annexation of my body, but I knew that I was lying to myself. My confusion had only grown. I had given up ownership, but Ingrid had felt so good. How could such a relinquishing bring pleasure? The question formed in my mind, spooked me, vanished, and circled back to haunt me.

Marianita burst through the swinging door carrying the huge silver platter as she did every night. As she lowered it to serve my mother, I recognized ox tongue, my father's favorite dish. For the rest of us it was inedible. For me the difficulty was increased by the fact that I was studying human sense receptors in science class and there, in a delicate sauce, was the tongue itself, succulent and plump.

To amuse myself, annoy my father, and avoid eating it, I approached my slice of tongue as if I were a surgeon preparing for an operation. With my knife I tried to isolate the papillae, the taste buds on the surface of the tongue. I narrated my steps to my siblings as if I were a lecturer: "Here you will see the buds," I said, and indicated them with the tip of my knife. "They are called buds because under a microscope they have the shape of a bud on a tree or a stem that will bloom in spring. Papillae can be found on many places of the body, not just the tongue. The skin, for example, has them embedded subcutaneously." Tim started to laugh. My father grew impatient and asked me to stop talking and "get down to business."

I hated the taste of tongue. I cut pieces of it into the smallest shapes, until I was eating specks. I moved rice around my plate to disguise what remained. To confuse matters further, I even ate a small piece of broccoli and let little bits of its greenery fall onto the pile of swirled food. My plate looked as if a tempest had struck it.

For that brief moment, I knew I couldn't continue. I decided I was going on strike. So what if ox tongue was my father's favorite dish? I didn't care that by not eating I was sealing my fate as a thin person forever. How this defiance was connected to my session with Ingrid I couldn't tell, but I knew that it was. Dad said, "Come on, Jon. A few more bites. Do it for your grandparents if not for me. They are as worried about you as we are."

I looked at him as if he were blackmailing me. "I don't like it, Dad. I'm not going to eat it," I said. This was the first time I had ever refused an outright order. It felt like treason.

"I see," he said, and shifted in his chair. "Okay, don't. Pass me your plate. I'll eat it." I knew I had disappointed him, but I passed it to him, glad to be rid of it, and he took what was left and passed it back. I watched him take mouthful after mouthful, and I was thrilled I didn't have the sickening taste and slippery feel of it in my mouth. I didn't understand how anyone could love that unless it was the only cut of meat that they could afford.

I left the table that night feeling proud of myself and larger for my rebellion. A new, expanded sense of self arose in me. Even at school the next day, I felt more sure. I knew that this change in me wasn't just about refusing to eat ox tongue.

For weeks after visiting Ingrid I avoided my mother. When she asked me her usual probing questions offering me "a penny for my thoughts", I gave nondescript answers and ignored her searching stares. I had never wanted to hide from her as badly as I did then. Clearly, she knew something was wrong. I felt guilty and burdened by the secret I was carrying. If Dad hadn't told me not to tell her, I would have blurted it out and hoped that she would forgive me, but I knew I had to avoid doing that at all costs. The repercussions would be massive and beyond my control.

One day after school I sensed that I couldn't postpone visiting her any longer. I would have to pretend that there were no barriers between us or she would get suspicious. Despite the forbidden subject, I wanted to feel the same attention and adoration I had always felt when I was younger, and so I knocked on her bedroom door. I didn't hear a reply, so I walked in. The pale blue bedcover embroidered with my parents' intertwined initials in dark blue florid script was pulled tight over the mattress.

"Mom?" I called out.

"I'm in here," she said. "Come in." I turned the corner, and she was sitting at her vanity in a blue satin slip with spaghetti straps facing the floor-to-ceiling mirrors. I took my usual position lying on my side on the small loveseat looking at her almost naked back. We made eye contact through the mirror.

For the first time in all of my visits to Mom's dressing room, her state of undress made me anxious. I wanted to stay with her, but I didn't want to watch as she chose her outfit and made herself up. Suddenly, after Ingrid, that felt too intimate, almost taboo. Maybe it had been acceptable when I was a boy, but the experience that I had had put an end to that—not to mention, I was withholding a lethal secret. I wanted to pretend that the nature of our bond hadn't changed, but the tension in my head told me that was wrong. If I wasn't careful, everything would spill out and I would be the cause of my parents' rupture, the dissolution of the family, or possibly something worse.

She went through the usual rituals of attending to her hair and makeup, choosing her bracelets, rings, and necklaces, and smoothing the hairs down on the hairpieces propped on their white heads in front of her. They formed the army she mustered each afternoon to prepare for the evening.

"I'm so glad you came to visit. I feel as if we haven't spoken to each other in months, What have you been thinking about, Jon?" she asked. My only thoughts were of silence, disappearance, and obfuscation.

In the past this standard opening question had been an invitation to spontaneously say what was on my mind. Sometimes I talked about what happened at school, and sometimes I didn't feel like saying anything. It had always felt to me that she wanted to know too much. Whenever I clammed up, she filled the gap. She told me where she had driven that day and the dress she had seen at the shop in Chappaqua that she wanted to buy. I followed her as she flitted from topic to topic absentmindedly. As she talked, she picked up the tall bottle of Calèche perfume from the glass tabletop and squirted it in the air around her.

"Jon, did you know that some women think that the best way to wear perfume is to spray it in front of you and walk into it? Otherwise, it is too intense. Too concentrated. Some women are wacky. Do you know how women choose men? They pay complete attention and draw pictures for themselves. He must be courtly and polite, handsome, of course, intellectually curious and curious about her, solicitous of her feelings, interested in the world and respectful of all women, able to grasp abstract ideas yet be a pragmatist. He must hold doors open for her and let her pass through them first. He must notice what she wears and how she combines her colors. He must be flattering about her appearance, or how will she know that he even noticed her? When we were in college the boys from Yale were exceptional. We always knew they looked at us, but we could never catch them doing it. That is how a man should be—not some leering, ogling Neanderthal." As she said this, she twisted around on the thin green velvet cushion on top of the white cast iron stool and gave me a stern, meaningful look. "I think you know who I'm talking about."

Through the enchanting fog of perfume and hairspray, her eyes drilled into me. I knew who she was describing. She had referred to him before as a "caveman" who pawed her when she hadn't invited it. Her favorite word for him and the behavior of men like him was *uncouth*.

"When you grow up I want you to be a gentleman whether you go to Yale or not." She stood up and smoothed down her slip. She slid open one of the giant white doors and touched each blouse until she found the one she wanted. I tried to imagine what combination of mood or whim made her select one over another, but it almost didn't matter what she picked because she looked stunning in all of them. Her eyes shone. She smiled warmly and broadly like the princess she had once been, the first Jewish Princess of the Aksarben Ball—Aksarben being Nebraska, her home state, spelled backwards. She kept the picture of herself in her long copper-colored gown on her dressing room table. It established beyond any doubt what a beautiful woman she was, and she reveled in the attention that her appearance brought from the men who swarmed around her. Flirting with them came so naturally to her that she did it without meaning to. When she lifted her chin, gave her luminous, compassionate smile that accompanied the hypnotic music of her jewelry, she convinced herself completely that her coyness was harmless and playful.

"Have you ever thought about going to school in Switzerland?" she asked out of the blue, as if the idea had just occurred to her. "Ellen Mitnick has offered many times to let you use their house as a home away from home if you wanted to give Eric's school a try. She means it. You could learn French and meet 'international' people. You could travel easily to Paris and London and explore Europe when there wasn't enough time to come home. You would have a European education. It might do you a world of good to get away from here for a while. Don't you think?" Her proposition startled me at first. I paused before answering as I recalled the town; the streets, the unfamiiar aromas in the air, the exotic everyday details of life.

"I loved Lausanne. But living there? Do you think it's a good idea?" I asked. At first her suggestion seemed farfetched. I was about to graduate from Adams and go to a New England prep school like the other boys. "It's so far from home," I added.

"True, but after a few months you'd be used to it and we would too. And then we'd have an excuse to come to Europe to visit you. I think you should give it a whirl," she said. "And Eric can help you settle in."

Her proposal struck me as slightly self-serving. I knew how much Mom liked Europe, not to mention the opportunity it would give her to spend more time with her best friend. If I were there, Dad would be hard-pressed to say no to her going.

Still, my father wouldn't be easy to convince. As it was he wasn't sure I was physically and emotionally strong enough to go to a boarding school let alone a private school three thousand miles away. He'd said to me that maybe I should go away to prep school when I was older and stronger, as if it were a destination I had been dreaming of. From what I heard about the pranks and ordeals that went on, prep school was an extension of Adams.

The thought of going to school so far away gave me mixed feelings. I imagined myself isolated in an Alpine tower, protected from Dad's strategies and Mom's ideas of the man I should become, but also cold and friendless. The advantage was that at that distance I wouldn't have to be so careful at keeping Ingrid a secret, and I could grow up at my own rate. What first sounded isolating began to feel more like a refuge when I thought about it. All of the other considerations—the school itself, the language, the Mitnicks—were trivial by comparison.

"It'd be so weird not living here, but I think I could do it. Do I have to stay for all of high school? Can I come back if I don't like it?" I asked.

"You can always come back. You know what Robert Frost said, don't you, dear?" she asked.

"No, no idea," I said.

"Home is a place where they have to take you in. We will always take you in. Always, darling."

She turned around to look at me as I struggled to remember Lausanne and Eric's school, École Nouvelle de la Suisse Romande. "So, what do you think? Should we talk to Dad about it tonight?" The transformation that had taken place in her appearance while she seemed to be chatting idly was breathtaking. The perfume she wore smelled like the blooming roses that she had planted in the lower gardens. Her shellacked blond hair was glowing and sprayed into frozen flicked-up waves. The gold earrings and blue stones in her brooch picked up the magnetism in her eyes. Her smile perfectly disguised the pixieness of her leonine will and manipulative power.

At dinner that night she brought up her new idea. Because she thought selling it to Dad would be required, she used her full arsenal of facial tactics, from stares to glancing away when he looked at her to sipping her wine and studying the bottom of her glass. He asked a few practical questions but seemed to not mind the proposition.

"Don't you think we should visit the school before we make a big decision like that?" he asked. "We didn't see much of it, and all we know is what Ellen says about it. Let's investigate it a little further. Maybe there are other graduates we could speak to in New York? Who sends their kids to a boarding school in Lausanne, Switzerland? Do you think you could hack it, Jon? It's a long way from home. I guess you could. You might make it there. Who knows? Lausanne might be a good place for you to land. Maybe you'll like it. I love the idea of your learning French. What do you think?"

There was something in the way he asked my opinion that made me believe that he was granting me a new level of respect. Perhaps he viewed me differently since my refusal to eat ox tongue. "I think I could," I answered.

In bed that night I thought of myself in Switzerland. There I was a different person, one with more gravity and seriousness, not a luftmensch drifting from village to village or wherever the wind carried him. My opinions would be clearer and well considered, not flighty. Without Mom or Dad to impose their desires, ideals, habits, and needs on me, I might have the chance to discover who I was and what I wanted to be. I would come into focus rather than being the mirror that reflected what people wanted to see of themselves.

This vision seduced me. There would be no McEnerys there to crush me or Ingrids paid to caress me or milkshakes that I couldn't stomach. I had survived all of that, and I was stronger. I knew I could become different there: hardened, self-protecting, and less naïve. And it was far away. Maybe I could become my real self.

*Part 2*

# chapter 7

O n the car ride from the Geneva airport to École Nouvelle, the
mood was tense. Dad wore his driving face—unblinking, lips
pursed, cheeks taut—on which it was impossible to read how great
the distance was or what kind of mission he was on. Mom focused
on her needlepoint of a gray-white unicorn prancing in a circular ring. She looked up occasionally to check the scenery before
turning her anxiety back to her lap-size tapestry. My excitement at
the new school and language conflicted with the sense that I was
being demoted. Switzerland might be a refuge, but it also felt like
a demotion to an overseas junior league from the varsity of a New
England boarding school. My weight hadn't increased enough to
keep me on the regular teenage track. I hoped that instead, far
away, out of sight, my situation might change, as if by magic.

As soon as we had discussed the possibility of my going to Switzerland that night at dinner, it had quickly become the obvious option.
By the time the application had been submitted and the deposit sent,
my parents and I were so convinced of its inevitability that they saw
no reason for me to visit the school again or learn more than what we
had read in the brochure or heard from Ellen Mitnick. It was a private
school that had a large coed day-student body and a small boarding
contingent that was only boys. Like all of the other students, I would
follow the program of the Maturité, the Swiss national exam, which
included Latin, Italian, English, French literature, Swiss history,
European history, mathematics, physics, chemistry, biology, and
philosophy. All classes were taught in French. There was no introduc-
tory period to ease foreigners into the language. It was the linguistic
equivalent of being thrown off the dock into a cold lake and calling it
a swimming lesson. This made me feel brave in a reckless way. In one
year of French I had barely progressed beyond regular verbs.

When Dad pulled into the little lane that led to the main school
building, he turned around to look at me with a meaningful expression,

as if to say, This is it, Jon. This is where you will make your mark. I looked at the strange buildings. They were faced in stucco darkened by years of grime. Some were private houses, and some were larger with more stories.

We drove into the gravel courtyard, and Dad pulled alongside the other cars. The scent of chestnut trees and autumn filled the air. Across from us was a large building that students much younger than I were running in and out of. To the side was another large building in the same Swiss style of curving shingled roof lines and Tudor fascia. "Follow me," Dad said, and gave us a hand signal that urged us to fall in behind him as he strode up its stone steps. He stopped briefly in the hallway to read the various signs on the doorways until he found the one that said PRESIDENT. My mother and I looked at each other but picked up the pace to walk into the president's office as closely behind him as possible.

Without any admission of a language barrier, my father said to the receptionist, "Please tell the president that I am here with my son Jonathan." As an aside he added to me in a stage whisper, "Remember to always meet the head guy right away. The decision maker." This was a tidbit of sales wisdom he had passed along to Tim and me many times as part of our general education. The receptionist looked up at Dad slightly bewildered.

"Do you has rendez-vous wees heem?" she asked.

"No, but please say that I would like to meet him and introduce my wife and son," he said.

"Un moment," she said, pronouncing words we could all understand.

"Go easy, Arnold," my mother said. "Maybe they're not used to American English."

We heard French conversation through the door and then a huge, sweet-faced man lumbered out and offered my father his giant hand. "Monsieur Le Pin," he said. "I am the President of Ecole Nouvelle. Be welcome here with us," he said, and invited us into his office without offering us seats. "So, Jonathan, we are so happy to invite you to our homes," he said to us in French in the Swiss accent I was beginning to recognize. I only understood a few words and had never heard my full name pronounced in French before. It sounded more Jewish than it ever had in English.

"Merci," I said. That was the only word I could muster that I was sure had no errors.

"Monsieur Buhler, is the chef of the boarding school. He will show you your new room," he added. I stared at my shoes instead of repeating "Merci."

My father said, "Belle école," to Le Pin. My mother, who spoke French fairly well, having learned a specialized vocabulary from her recipes, added, "Vous avez beaucoup d'arbres à l'école," gesturing awkwardly toward the trees outside the window. After a few moments another heavyset man, this one with wispy hair and a faint mustache, arrived.

"Monsieur Buehler," he said, offering his hand. Like Le Pin, he had a strange accent that sounded to my ear as if French wasn't his native language. "I am the head of the boarding school. Suivez-moi," he said, extending his arm toward the door. We followed him up two flights of stairs to the top floor. My single room was to the right, with a window shaped like a porthole. "I hope you will be comfortable here with us," he said in English, nodded, and left. He seemed formal but not unkind.

I looked around the room. It was strange to think that this would be my new home. Everything about it was blank. There were no posters on the wall or ceiling, no orange rug on the floor or books on the shelves. "Let's roll up our sleeves and get to work," my mother said. I lifted the blue suitcase onto the bed as she hung the clothes in the wardrobe. I put my Dylan Thomas *Collected Poems* and Ferlinghetti's *Coney Island of the Mind* on the shelf. The most critical part was setting up the stereo that was a going-away present from my parents. I placed the speakers on the desk, unlocked the arm, and plugged it in. It made a rasping noise as I brushed my thumb across the needle. That was the happiest sound of the day. It meant that I would not be separated from my records. Without them filed neatly next to the bed, I couldn't imagine how I would get started in a world where I knew no one and didn't speak the language.

I watched my mother organizing my shirts and jackets. She smoothed the shoulders as if I were wearing them and she was fussing over me. My father sat in the study chair examining a map of the city to find directions to the Mitnicks' house, as we had been invited to dinner. The snapshots of my parents at their separate activities in different frames registered in me as a touchstone that I could refer back to and derive comfort from when the separation became difficult. Their simple chores temporarily removed the painful memories of their encroachments. They were doing the things that I imagined normal parents did. We were mutually respectful. No boundaries were crossed.

As soon as Mom finished, Dad said, "It's time to go. They live so close to here, you can go there anytime."

"You know they're dying to get to know you better, Jon," Mom added. "They want to be your Swiss parents. Isn't that terrific?" she asked. I nodded, completely unconvinced. Maybe one set of parents was enough, I thought.


"Jonny, you're here!" Ellen said, opening the front door. "It feels like we've been waiting for you to come for years. That's how long it took me to convince Jeannie to send you to us." We followed her in and down the marble steps. Nathan sat in a heap on the couch. In spite of his giant girth and height, he stood up as soon as we approached. Next to him I felt like a toddler.

"Welcome to Lausanne, Jonny. Listen to me," Nathan said sternly as he squished my hand. "You are always welcome here." Why did they call me Jonny? I wondered. Maybe Eric had something to do with it. I looked around for him, but he wasn't in the room.

"Eric!" Ellen shouted up the stairs. Silence. "Eric!" she shouted again. "Jonny's here." No reply. "He'll be down in a minute," she said, reassuring us. "How is your room at school?" she asked.

"We fixed it up a little, and it's comfortable. Not large but comfortable," my mother answered.

When we sat down in the dining room Eric still hadn't appeared. Ellen looked at me as if I might know the reason for his absence. A butler in a white jacket appeared out of the side door and set a plate down in front of me. Every square inch of it held several layers of food. The largest portion was beets, a vegetable I hated. I used my fork to push the other food away from them so it wouldn't be stained that purple livid color. Eric shuffled in and sat next to me.

"Look, he doesn't eat beets," he said immediately, as if he had already found something wrong with me.

"You don't like beets, Jonny? Why not?" Nathan asked me as though he genuinely cared about the answer.

"It reminds me of borscht," I said. "And I don't like borscht." Nathan gave me an uncomprehending look.

"Arnold, he doesn't like borscht? What do you feed him?" he asked with a sneer that I soon realized was semipermanent.

"Mostly, he eats steak, Nathan. We try and get him to eat other food, but the doctor said he has a small stomach. So we let him eat pretty much what he wants. It doesn't do any good to push him," my father added. "If anything, it's worse." Dad was making up the medical information on the spot. Although I had stood up to his pushing me to eat, dinner at the Mitnicks' didn't feel like the right time to protest, so I forced myself to eat as much as I could, except for the beets.

"Eric, do you know any of the teachers I'll have?" I asked, hoping to break up his staring at me. He pretended he hadn't heard me.

"Eric, you could at least answer his question?" Ellen said.

"No idea," he answered. He chewed his food indifferently and barely looked at me or his parents.

"Can't you give him a clue, Eric?" she asked him.

"Nope. I don't know," he said.

When the white-jacketed waiter came back into the dining room to remove the plates, he looked at mine and then, seeing how much was left, at me. "Bring me his plate, Patrick. Where's Wolfy?" Nathan asked, looking for their enormous black German shepherd. Wolfy, on recognizing his name and knowing that it was somehow related to food, lifted his big head off the carpet and nuzzled Nathan's leg.

"Here, my brave boy. Look what Daddy's brought you," he said, feeding my leftovers between the dog's giant slobbering fangs. "Who's a hungry boy?" he asked, knowing it wasn't me.

That night I slept in my new room at school for the first time. Before turning off the light I listened to Dylan singing "Like a Rolling Stone." Its familiar lonesome chorus felt custom-made for me. "No direction home. A complete unknown" summed up my new status. But then I thought, if I could learn to speak French, master new subjects, and escape my parents' intrusions, wouldn't it all be worth it?

The next morning I met them for breakfast and then they drove me back to school to say good-bye. As we drove up the last hill we noticed a curious-looking church that we hadn't seen when we arrived the day before. "What kind of church is that? Does anybody know?" Mom asked. It had giant stained-glass bulbs growing out of a sturdy wooden body like the buildings in the Kremlin that I had seen in photos from *Life* magazine.

"It's Swiss Orthodox, I'm pretty sure," my father said, pulling the car to the curb and stopping. "Look at the onion shapes. That's a clear sign. Maybe this means that you'll become a monk, Jon." He looked back at me over his shoulder and grinned, amused that anyone might consider him an authority on foreign church architecture or who was destined for the monastery. What scared me was that as an extension of my luftmensch status, he was already worried about my place in the working world. Before referring to me as a monk, he had also tried me out as a headwaiter or maître d' in my Adams jacket and tie.

Dad parked in the courtyard. He opened the door to let me out and gave me a bear hug. "I can imagine a big future for you here. Next time I see you, you'll be fluent in French and I'll still be doing sign language," he said.

Mom had tears in her eyes. She hugged me skittishly and pulled away. "Let Ellen take care of you. She promised me that she would do that for you, for me." So she wouldn't fall apart, she gave me a peck on the cheek and rushed back to the car.

Dad stood beside me for another minute. "Here," he said. "These may be useful to you. We won't be needing them." He crumpled five Swiss franc notes into my hand.

I went back into the main building to M. Buehler's office for the coupon that I needed to buy my school books. He gave me a long explanation of what I was supposed to do, of which I only understood enough to know that I had to go to a bookstore named Payot on the rue de Bourg. He handed me a list of titles. I read through them and didn't recognize any of the authors or publishers. At the bottom of the hill I took the trolley downtown and got off at Place Saint-François. I saw the big sign PAYOT on a building that looked as if it would be a church if it were relocated to the New York suburbs. I handed my coupon to a clerk, who returned with a giant bag of textbooks. Weighted down, I walked back up the little pedestrian shopping street gazing into the shop windows. I stopped in front of the record store and saw album covers featuring Jimi Hendrix, Bob Dylan, and Fleetwood Mac with the familiar titles but different images.

As I hiked back up the hill to school, I stopped at the church that I now thought of as the Swiss Orthodox, as Dad had named it. My bag of books was heavy, so I set it on the ground at the entrance to the lane. Behind me I heard a commotion and turned around. There were two giant mounds of colored plastic strips almost thirty feet high in the courtyard of the first building. Around the larger piles were several smaller ones of similar colors. Men in knee-length blue coats milled around giving orders to one another that no one obeyed. It was like a Marx Brothers skit. There was a lot of shouting and no apparent leader. There was clearly something peculiar about these men. An instinct told me not to stare at them, but I couldn't help myself. They all seemed to suffer from some type of physical deformity. As I passed them, they watched me, went back to work, and then stopped again to stare at me too as if they weren't sure whether I was real or they had imagined me. "Where are you from?" one of them asked me brusquely using simple words without articles. Then another asked me the same question, and so did another. I answered, "New York," over and over and then, "Les Etats Unis." Each one wanted to ask me the same question to hear the answer for himself. Secondhand knowledge wasn't sufficient. Each time I gave the punch line, the questioner smiled as though my country and state, my identity, provided him with release from the tedium of his days sorting plastic strips into colors. When I walked away I heard them repeat, "New York," "New York," over and over, as if they were revelations that built into something bigger, a glimpse into another world, one of excitement and mystery, tantalizing cities and panoramas. Hearing the echoes as I walked into the school courtyard, I felt giddy that I was memorable even if they were mentally deficient. The four-color brochure the school had sent us didn't identify the other buildings on the lane and certainly didn't mention that there was an asylum of some type virtually on its doorstep.

When I returned to my small perch of a room I studied each book that I had bought and tried to imagine how the classes would be. In my mind I pictured them like the small classes at Adams but in French, except that there would be girls giggling at my poor pronunciation and grammar.

I put on Jimi Hendrix's "Castles Made of Sand" and listened to him play those ringing, bending chords. The solo had a transporting, hallucinatory effect. I could feel the notes bunch up in me and then slide away as if I had drunk a powerful elixir that made my head and stomach woozy. The potion was strong, strong enough to distract me from the potential embarrassment of speaking French in class.


That night I met the other boys on my hall for the first time. Our advisor, M. Montheil, had invited all eight of us to a restaurant that featured Swiss specialties. Aside from cheese fondue that I had shared with my brothers and sister on our family ski trips, I was completely ignorant of Swiss cuisine, so I prepared myself for the worst—unrecognizable animal parts, mysterious sauces and stews.

Montheil greeted me at the bottom of the stairs and shook my hand. He was an older, dignified man with a gray crew cut who wore rimless glasses. Montheil had been teaching history at the school for more than thirty years, he told us later. As each boy came down the staircase he shook his hand and scrutinized him. Most of the group were Swiss, although a few of them had Swiss-German accents like Mr. Buehler's. They wore blazers with polished buttons and creased gabardine slacks and loafers with tassels. They could have been mistaken for a group of private bankers in training.

In the van, Montheil announced that he had ordered a special dinner for us called raclette. At the restaurant we sat around a small table with a communal cooking stove in the center, an electric table-top broiler. On big plates in front of us was an assortment of foods to combine on triangular metal spoons and broil under the coils: air-dried beef from the Jura Mountains, raclette cheese, and creamy, boiled potatoes. After they melted together in the heat they were eaten with briny pickles and onions. Montheil demonstrated how it was done for those of us who hadn't tried it before.

As soon as I had my first spoonful I thought it was the most delicious combination of flavors I had ever tasted. To not lose time, I prepared the next helping as I ate the first one. It looked like the other boys were as obsessed by their next mouthful as I was. There was no time for conversation. Yet when the others had stopped eating, I kept preparing more until I noticed them staring at me, apparently mystified as to how such a small boy could pack so much in.

Unlike my dinner the night before at the Mitnicks', my first raclette stood out as one of the great meals of my life. Not only did I love the flavors, I liked the amazement of Montheil and the others over my performance. The food didn't seem to fill me up. I kept eating and could think of no reason to stop.

"Where is he hiding all of that?" Montheil asked with a wry smile. He looked from boy to boy for an answer.

"Maybe he is slipping them in his jockeys?" Andre, the glib, slick one with gelled hair from Geneva, said.

Serge, a dark-faced, slightly overweight boy who wore a gold signet ring carved with a family crest, said in English, "Maybe he never tasted anything that good before." He smiled at me, and I nodded because it was true. It was the most delicious food I had ever eaten, and in one sitting I was countering a lifetime of criticisms regarding my size. Although I only had a few more spoonfuls than the rest of them, the five minutes of awe I inspired lasted far longer.

Feeling expansive and generous as we climbed the stairs, I invited Serge to my room. I showed him the covers of *Highway 61 Revisited* and *The Freewheelin' Bob Dylan*.

"Which one do you prefer?" I asked. He took them from me and studied the change in Dylan's face from a boyish man strolling a snowy Greenwich Village street with his girlfriend, indifferent to the camera, to a taunting sphinx who dared the lens to come any closer.

"I don't know them. Play me the one you like. Perhaps I've heard of him. Who is he?" he asked. "Mostly I listen to opera. Is that him singing? He has a terrible voice," he said after hearing only one line. "How can you listen to that?"

"It's the lyrics that interest me most I guess, but the voice goes with them," I said.

"Oh, I see," he said in a way that indicated he didn't. He stood up, held out his hand to shake mine, and said in a formal, distant way, "Bonne nuit."

"Bonne nuit," I echoed, knowing that we would never be friends. But even that didn't disturb the delicious memory of the burnt raclette cheese that I scraped off the spoon and mixed with salty meat and soft potatoes.


The first few weeks of classes were arduous. As I tried to simultaneously translate words and tenses from my teachers' monologues while still absorbing the information, my head started to hurt. I fell further behind with each sentence, as the other students, especially the girls, took notes. By midmorning I had a severe headache and yearned for the morning-break bell to ring. When it did, all of the classrooms emptied and silently I joined the jabbering students on the stairs to the courtyard. Like clockwork, the pastry van from the local boulangerie drove in through the pillars, kicking up pebbles and dust. The driver lifted the side panel, revealing the freshly baked pastries: croissants, brioches, and pains au chocolat. Biting into the soft flaky dough made me forget the agonies of trying to understand French.

Andre and Serge stood talking animatedly in a group with some of the other boys from Geneva. I hovered near them, struggling to understand their weekend boating plans on the lake, with nothing to add myself. They used an entirely different vocabulary from the one in the classroom. I quickly gave up trying to follow their conversation when I heard two girls speaking English behind me. I turned. Beyond the girls, behind the school's pillars, I glimpsed the men from the asylum staring at the crowds of students. Their jarring appearance emboldened me with something to say: "Don't they put you off?" I asked Erica, who I sat next to in French class. She had black glistening curls that reached down to the middle of her back. She was talking to Birgitta, a tall Swedish girl who never said a word. They wore identical knee-length, cable-knit sweaters, crisp white blouses, and slacks. They didn't resemble the girls I had known in dancing class. In spite of the color in their cheeks and their lively eyes, it seemed as if their youth was missing. They had a mature bearing, with nothing casual about them. Erica turned toward me as if I was as much an intruder as the men from the asylum. "We're so used to them we don't even notice them anymore, do we?" Birgitta nodded, and then they walked away arm in arm as if I had brought up a distasteful subject.

The next day at lunch I looked for Birgitta and Erica in the dining room, but they were nowhere to be seen, so I sat with the usual group from my hall. "Do any of you know where the others go?" I asked them. They looked at me and then one another and shrugged. Clearly, the question didn't interest them. My lunch plans changed the next day. Erica and Birgitta were in my class before lunch, and this time, rather than heading to the dining room, I followed them at a safe distance, as they left school and walked down the hill to the main street. They turned into the Café de la Rose, a nondescript establishment, and a moment later I did as well.

Inside, the jukebox was playing King Crimson, interrupted by the bells and gongs of several pinball machines. I spotted Birgitta and Erica, giggling, pointing, and smoking cigarettes, as was everyone else in the packed room. They were surrounded by a group of students that I vaguely recognized from the school court-yard. The guys were big and sloppy, hair uncombed, pockets turned out, laughing, pushing one another, playing foosball, shouting and cursing in languages I couldn't identify. They were all eating ham sandwiches on long sections of buttered baguette, and from what I could decipher, they were making jokes about smoking hash and coughing enthusiastically as if it were the most important ritual of their lunch routine.

"Do you come here every day?" I asked Erica and Birgitta hesi-tantly. They looked at each other as if they needed to confer before answering the question. A giant redheaded boy in a floor-length blue military jacket interjected himself before they could answer and said, "Who is he? How did he find his way here? Who are you? *Nouvel eleve?*" A new student? he asked. I didn't believe that Emily and Birgitta could be friends with someone as scruffy as he was.

I started to say, "C'est la première fois que," to tell him this was my first visit.

"Speak English," he said, interrupting. "We all do. Yves, come here," he shouted to an older boy with bad skin and a sweet pixie-ish smile. "Who are you and where are you from? Why are you here? Exiled? Most of us are exiles, whether we live with our families or not," he said.

"Exiles, Axel? That's bullshit. Really we're just immigrants," Yves said.

"I never thought of it that way, but maybe I'm an exile too," I said. "Where are all these people from?"

"We're from all over. Turkey. Greece. Our families came to Switzer-land for different reasons, and we wound up at La Rose. *Comme tu vois,*" he said, looking around the loud room as though he was the host and smiling for his audience. "And you?" he asked. "What's your excuse?"

"My parents thought it would be safer for me to come to school in Switzerland than an American school, so they sent me here. Maybe not an exile but close," I said.

"So refugee from what, I won't ask. Stick with us," he added. "Hash?" he asked, digging in his pocket. He showed me a tiny crinkled piece of tinfoil and handed it to me. I stared at it, not sure what to do with it. *"Viens, je vais te montrer,"* he said, leading me to one of the tables. He took out his lighter, which featured Jim Morrison's scowling face and naked torso in a crucifixion pose, and heated the tinfoil for a second before crumbing the hash onto rolling paper, mixing it with tobacco, and twisting it up between his fingers. He stuck a cardboard filter he'd rolled into the fat end. "Voilà," he said. *"Pour toi.* Your first hash joint, obviously. Take it easy. It's the Afghani black that has little opium flakes in it, or so they tell us."

The noise, the jukebox, and hearing so much English convinced me that the Café de la Rose would be my home away from home. And so it was. In the days that followed, Erica and Birgitta, Axel and Yves helped me through the classes, and so did the hash that one or the other of them gave me. At first it was free, but then they started to charge me random prices for the bits of Lebanese or Afghani that they broke off and stuck in my pocket.

At the end of the day I'd open the little window in my room, light the joint, and blow the smoke into the chestnut leaves. Home was so far away. I missed all of it—my parents, my brothers and sister. I missed Sinbad, the big black Newfoundland dog Danny had talked my parents into getting for him when he said he had no one to play with. I missed Marianita, her silver platter and her golden tooth. I played my records to break down the distances and closed my eyes and imagined what they were doing and the rooms they were in.

Each week I wrote a letter home that attempted to describe my new life. I threw in new French words I'd learned to impress them with my progress and other words from the books in English I read on my own, even lines of Dylan Thomas poems that came back to me from having heard them so many times. But I was careful to not tell them about my homesickness. I wanted them to think I was brave and independent, especially my mother. Confessing how much I missed them would make me vulnerable to more questions, ones I knew I didn't want to answer, like who are your friends and what do you do with them? Do you have a girlfriend yet?

Dad added me to the recipient list of the weekly newsletter he dictated to Jo and circulated to his mother in Miami Beach, the grandparents in Omaha, and the rest of the family. That told me where they had been and what they had done, but much was omitted. Were Danny and Eileen, now seven and nine, eating grown-up food? How would Tim decide what prep school he would go to? Dad's letters were a list of facts and places that made me yearn to be back there so I could see it all for myself, understand it in my own way, and describe it as I saw it. They made me want to give up and return home, but I knew I couldn't do that so I decided to call Ellen Mitnick the next morning. She picked up on the first ring. "Jonny! I was wondering how long it would take for you to call. How are you doing? Why don't you come over and spend the weekend with us?" Those were the sweetest words I had heard since my arrival.

# chapter 8

The following Saturday after classes finished at noon Ellen opened the door and smothered me in kisses. "Tell me everything, Jonny," she said, leading me to the living room sofa that was large enough to fill a bank lobby. "How are your teachers? Let's start there."

"Montheil is a kind man," I answered, launching into it as if I hadn't confided in anyone for weeks. "He speaks slowly, so I can understand almost every word, and he makes strong connections between the world and Switzerland, how the small country soaked up the themes of the rest of Europe." I noticed that Ellen was staring out the window, hardly listening to my answer. When she saw that I had noticed how distracted she was, she said, "Jeannie would be so proud of you. Let's call her tomorrow, darling, shall we? You can talk as long as you want. Nathan doesn't care about phone bills. He lives more on the phone than he lives with me," she said, searching my face for a sign that I recognized her predicament.

Every time she called me "darling" it felt more like a dismissal than an endearment. "You know, Jonny, you're like a second son to me. I love you so much, darling." She looked at me with her bright ingot eyes in her freckled face with clumps of red hair piled on her head, and all I could think was, How could she say that? She barely knew me except as the son of her close friend. So maybe I was her son by extension? Was that what she meant? Or the son of her closest friend was the same as her own? These were new concepts of what family meant, but I wanted to believe each one for as long as I could. I tried to imagine what being her son would be like but it felt strange, like getting used to a friend's lazy eye. Between effusions her attention wandered back to the windows, as if she were trying to see something in the lake, far below the surface.

"How's Bordas?" she asked. "Eric had a horrible class with him his first year. He was a typical Swiss disciplinarian. I never saw him smile. Do you have him?"

"He's my French teacher. He's so strict. If you don't answer his question precisely as it's written in the textbook, if you leave any word out, he scolds you. The other day we were reading Pascal and considering his definition of man as a reed, but as a reed that thinks. He called on me. 'Vells, what is Pascal's definition of man?' I couldn't remember the French word for 'reed.' I said something like 'Man is defined by thinking.' 'But a thinking what?' he asked. I blanked on the word. I looked around for help, but my classmates were all too scared of Bordas. The next thing I knew I was struck on the forehead by something sharp. I didn't realize what'd happened until I saw the piece of chalk he'd thrown rolling on the floor. 'Vells, tu es un espece de petit crapeau,' he said. My teacher had called me a species of miniature toad. I guess that was what he thought I was.

Ellen was staring out the window again. Drowning in her thoughts, she said nothing. Her face expressed no sympathy for Bordas's assault on me. Even the other students in the class had shown more understanding, clearly shocked by what their teacher had done. "Would you like to take a shower?" Ellen asked suddenly. "I bet it would be nice to have your own bathroom, wouldn't it?"

"Yes, thank you. Privacy would be nice," I said.

While I was drying myself off, I could hear a thumping beat through the floorboards of the old house. I put my clothes on quickly and walked down the hall toward the music. The bass guitar and drum boomed through the door, so I knocked loudly and then heard Eric's voice shouting at me to come in. When I entered he held up the cover of *Let It Bleed* by the Rolling Stones with its multitiered birthday cake about to be lowered onto a vinyl platter. Moving his head and upper body in time to "Midnight Rambler," pounding his feet on the floor as if he were trudging through a muddy field in high boots, he sat behind his desk, which was piled up with textbooks. Eric was tall, with his father's dark, curly hair, and when he hinged forward on the beat, I could see how thin it was, barely covering his scalp.

I sat down on the chair facing him as he rocked back and forth to the music. It was as if he didn't see me. He was in a trance. I squirmed and tried to think of something to say. "When's your first exam?" I asked him. The guitar chords covered his silence. He held up the album jacket again.

"Just out," he said.

"What is the best record store in Lausanne? I only saw the one on rue de Bourg. Is that where you got it?" I asked him. Again he didn't respond. I wasn't sure whether I should leave or not. "Do you know Axel and Yves?" I asked, thinking he might have met them as they were in the grade below him. He paused for a second, looked straight at me with his popping eyes as if I had asked something particularly stupid.

"No, should I?" he answered with annoyance.

I racked my brain for conversation. What would make Eric pay attention to me, give me stature in his eyes, make me as mature as he was? Before I knew what I was saying, I blurted out, "Dad sent me to a prostitute last spring. She was Swedish. Her name was Ingrid." Suddenly he stopped moving, turned the volume down, and lifted the needle.

"What did you say? Say that again. What did Arnold do?"

"He sent me to Ingrid. She lives on Sixty-Eighth Street. She's Swedish and had dark hair tied back with a yellow scarf. Did you know some Swedish girls weren't blondes?"

"Wait, wait a second, your father sent you to a hooker? Are you kidding me? And he gave you the money? What did she do to you? Tell me every detail. Don't leave anything out."

"Dad made the appointment for me and gave me a hundred-dollar bill. He didn't tell me much about her before I met her, so I didn't know what to expect."

"How did she look? What did she say to you?"

"You know, she asked the usual questions. Did I like sports? Did we have any pets? Stuff like that. She was pretty. No, she was cute. She had jet-black hair. Did you know that some Swedish girls have black hair?" I asked him again.

"Yeah, of course they do. Some must. What did she do to you?" he asked.

"She took my clothes off," I said.

"You mean that's it?" he asked. "She undressed you? Then what? Did she give you a bath? Come on, Jonny. I want details. Did she suck your dick?"

"Yes, a little," I said, already regretting that I had brought Ingrid up.

"Look, Jonny. You can't tell me just a little of this and that and then hold out on me. It's not kosher. Either you tell me the whole thing or you shouldn't have brought it up in the first place. So what else did she do? Did you fuck her? You're probably not old enough. How old are you, anyway? You look like you're eleven. So did you? Man, your dad is the greatest. Mine wouldn't ever do that for me. So what did she feel like?" he asked. Thinking of Nathan in a carnal position made me squirm.

"She felt perfect," I said, hoping that would shut him up.

"Did she let you touch her tits? Between her legs?" he asked. Now he was leaning forward toward me over the stacks of books and albums. His jaw looked like it was chewing something.

"She took my hands and moved them around her body. You can't tell anyone," I said. It felt like I had started a little fire that I thought I could control and then the whole forest was suddenly burning. "I could get in big trouble if someone else finds out."

"Yeah, don't worry about it," he said. "Man, you're lucky."

He fixed his eyes on me and didn't blink. He was trying to decide whether I had made the whole thing up to get his attention. His eyes sparkled and his jaw was stuck open. As the information sank in, I could tell he was looking at me differently, as though reassessing my value. He stared at me for a long second as he put "Midnight Rambler" back on and turned the volume up even louder than it had been before.

After the first guitar chords crashed out of the speakers and he turned away, my impulse was to flee as soon as he blinked, but that didn't happen for several awkward, miserable moments. When he put his head down into the music, I stood up and rushed for the door. The hall felt like a tunnel. I threw myself down on the bed and lay there rigid with dread, asking myself how I could have told Eric about Ingrid when I hadn't even told Tim. Maybe it was the safety that distance from home provided. Maybe I was that desperate. Was that the only way I could get him to notice me? My mouth was stale. I wanted to evaporate or sleep for days in my misery. I had handed Eric the most vulnerable part of myself, and I had no idea what he would do with it. I had never felt as unsafe in my life, as naked as I did at that moment, and all I could think of was how to disappear from that room and that house.

I must have fallen asleep because the next thing I heard was the sound of a bell. At first I wasn't sure if it was part of a dream, and then I realized it was the bell for dinner that the Mitnicks used. Sluggishly, I stood up and patted my hair down in the mirror. Maybe what had happened with Eric was a dream? Ellen waited for me at the bottom of the stairs.

"Why don't you call home now, darling?" she asked. She led me to the study, which housed a collection of at least twenty pairs of bronzed hands reaching up, and closed the door after showing me how to dial the overseas code. My mother picked up and said, "Hello, dear." As soon as I heard her voice I was transported back to the closeness of her dressing room. Compared with the giant house I was in, with its own elevator and priceless art, it felt warm and manageable.

"Where are you? Is everything all right?" she asked with alarm as she always did when I called unexpectedly.

"I'm at the Mitnicks' for the weekend. Don't worry about how much it costs. They said it was all right to call. How are you? I miss you a lot," I said. Through the interference on the line I could hear Sinbad bark in the background. When my mother put her hand over the receiver and told Dad that it was me, word spread through the house and all my siblings rushed to grab the phone to talk to me at once. My home's gravitational pull reached across the ocean with a grasping hand like one of the bronze ones on the black leather desk in front of me. Switzerland was a desolate place. I wanted to go home if for no other reason than that I already knew where the traps were.

Reluctantly, I hung up and went into the dining room, where Eric, Ellen, and Nathan sat waiting for me. They grumbled from time to time but barely spoke to one another. Wolfy sat at Nathan's feet, only lifting his giant black head when he thought table scraps were about to be fed to him. A plate was set in front of me with food hanging off the edges. I felt defeated by it even before I lifted my fork. My hard-won principle of taking only as much food as I could eat was foiled by the plate that had been prepared for me in the kitchen: heaps of boiled potatoes and entangled broccoli branches and a giant slab of meat. At that moment I didn't care whether I stuck to my eating principles or not. My appetite abandoned me and I pushed the food around my plate as I used to do before the big day when I had refused to eat more than I wanted. Nathan speared a big piece off my plate to dangle in front of Wolfy.

On Sunday Eric's best friends spent the day at the house and gave it a livelier atmosphere. Per-Henrik (or P.-H.) was a tall, blond, good-looking Swede in Eric's class, as was Assene, a stocky Bulgarian. The two of them formed Eric's close-knit circle and were inseparable. They spent the afternoon in Eric's room spinning fantasies of film plots and other projects, the kind of young men who were always mapping out speculative plans for the future together, not because they might actually happen but because they served as templates for their practical imaginations.

The door to Eric's room was open, and I stood by it as if the previous day's humiliation hadn't happened. P.-H. sat by the open window, and the breeze lifted his light hair. Assene sprawled on the floor in a dead man's pose, while Eric had his feet up on the desk. When Eric saw me lingering at the door, he waved me in and pointed to a chair.

"Jonny, to bring you up to speed," Eric said. "We're working on a screenplay about Switzerland during World War II. Officially, the country was neutral but unofficially they let Nazi trains pass through the Swiss German areas and banked gold that the Nazis stole from the Jews in the camps. If you want, you can add something. Otherwise, be quiet."

"Did you find that book *Letters to Suzanne* I told you about? It's in the library," Eric, clearly the team's unofficial captain, asked Assene.

"I looked through it but didn't take it out. I don't think we need it."

"Well, we know the Swiss turned thousands of Jews and refugees away from their borders before and during the war. We know they stamped "J" in their passports and stuck their money in banks in Geneva and Zurich. We know they bought hundreds of thousands of pieces of Melmer gold stolen from Holocaust victims. We know they let Nazi trains pass through their borders. How do we turn it into a story?" Eric asked.

The three looked at one another sourly. Beyond setting their film in Nazi-sympathizing, German-speaking Switzerland during World War II, they had no further ideas.

"What if one of the Nazi-leaning colonels in the Swiss Armed Forces has a German Jewish wife who is trying to smuggle her family in. Would that work?" P.-H. finally asked. The others shrugged.

"What do you think, Jonny?" Eric asked me.

"That sounds like a good twist. Maybe you can use it?" I said.

Speculation and story line reached a dead end. They scribbled notes in their little notebooks and idly turned the pages of their reference books.

"Assene, get that book for us. Maybe it'll give us another idea. Hey, guys, you know what Jonny's dad did?" Eric asked. They looked up. I felt nauseous immediately. Before Eric said another word, I knew what was coming.

"What did he do?" P.-H. asked.

"You won't believe this," Eric said. "His dad gave him the money and sent him to a hooker. Can you believe that? Maybe we should work it into the screenplay somehow?"

"I've heard of fathers doing this before, but it's rare even in Bulgaria. How was she, Jonny? Aren't you a little young for that? In my country at least the father waits until the boy is thirteen. I didn't know fathers did this to their sons in America. Are you thirteen yet?" Assene asked in a benevolent voice.

"I'm almost sixteen!" I said.

"Oh, well, that's okay then. So tell us. What was she like?"

"Tell them what you told me yesterday. Don't leave anything out," Eric said. In a monotone I repeated what I had told Eric.

"Get to the sex part," Eric said. "Tell them what you told me."

"I don't want to." I stared at the floor. "You tell them."

"Eric, leave the poor kid alone. He doesn't have to tell us if he doesn't want to. We can make it up for ourselves," Assene said.

"She unzipped your fly and put her hand around your dick, right?" Eric asked me.

"No, that's not what happened. She kissed me on the cheek and then took me by the hand and made me sit down on the bed. Then she kneeled down and started untying my shoes. Then she unbuckled my belt and took off my socks. That's all I'm going to say, Eric," I said.

"Jonny, you're really holding out on us here. Why are you being so tricky?" he asked. Pointing to P.-H. and Assene, he said, "They can't wait to hear the rest of the story. Tell them, did she take her yellow scarf off when she sucked you?"

I stood up to leave. Assene and P.-H. watched me. They remained sprawled where they'd been when I had entered. Clearly, they felt sorry for me—but not as sorry as I felt for myself. Betrayed, mortified, enraged, nauseous. I couldn't tell which was the strongest feeling. I walked back down the hallway, which now felt like an Alpine trail going straight down to hell.

When I got to my room I lay down on the bed. I closed my eyes to block out what had just happened, and an image of a playing card came into my mind. It had two positions. Held flat into the light between my fingertips it was thin and as sharp as a razor blade, a weapon of thinness. It concealed its identity perfectly. It didn't show its rank, suit, or color. When it was tilted face up, all was revealed, the information immediately accessible. In my daydream I pivoted the card into and out of the light as it changed from one position to the other. I imagined myself as the card. On the one hand I was thin, reduced and hard, vigilant and quiet, inaccessible. In the other position I was open-hearted and candid. I would say anything to anyone for any reason without giving a thought to the risk. I was completely open and trusting.

The image as I pictured it turned itself over and spiraled as I played with its different positions; half-open, three quarters open, entirely flat, and nearly invisible in the light. If I had grasped the possible risks before going into Eric's room, I might have spared myself the painful scene and the betrayal that followed. I should have armed myself, knowing that Eric was not to be trusted, instead of entering unprepared. Or I should have not gone in at all, reduced to my thinnest, most inscrutable self.

I decided that even with the benefits of my own shower, better food, and being able to call home, I would not be returning anytime soon for another weekend at the Mitnicks'. There were other kids to make friends with and a chance that they might be less aggressive.

Although some classes lasted until noon, Saturday always felt like a holiday. Teachers were in a good mood, there were no tests, and the students were already planning their weekends. For the few boarders who didn't go home on the weekend to Geneva, or even as far away as Basel, it was a chance to wander around the town and have an ice cream sundae at the Mövenpick restaurant that had just opened near the university.

After the midday bell the school was mostly deserted. Although a proctor might show his face occasionally, he didn't take his job very seriously, and as a result there was little oversight. Kids came and went as they pleased and stayed up all night if they wanted to. Every few months there was another dinner on Saturday night with M. Montheil, except without raclette—a treat unfortunately reserved only for the first dinner. We had dances with one of the girls' schools around Lausanne from time to time, but aside from those infrequent events, there were no scheduled activities.

As a result the weekends were ruled by different gangs. The Turks, who were not both Turkish, were the ones I feared most. They held themselves in high esteem and were always smartly dressed in clean white creased shirts and pressed tan slacks with blue blazers whose gold buttons were always gleaming. Yarak, the dominant one, was the son of a Turkish millionaire. With a gangster's solid body, he was thickset, more a man than a boy. He looked at least ten years older than he was and had cheeks that were always dark, suggesting to me that he needed to shave more than once a day. School gossip indicated that he was quick to use his fists. Mohammed, his henchman, was Persian, and according to the same school gossip his father was a member of SAVAK, the shah of Iran's notoriously brutal secret police. Gaunt and over six feet tall, he wore his belt cinched at the bottom of his rib cage, making his pants too short for his scuffed black lace-up shoes. He had a haunted look that made me wonder what torture he had seen and what secrets he had to keep. Humming and mouthing words to himself, he was in communication with a ghostly inner self that was both spontaneously violent and sickly sweet. A penetrating sadness enveloped him. He almost never spoke, and hid his awkwardness with a high-pitched giggle.

At dinner one Saturday night, Yarak and Mohammed sat down on either side of me. "So, isn't your President Nixon a great man?" Yarak asked.

"No, he isn't, and Kissinger isn't either," I said. "They're attacking innocent people who have done nothing to them." Sensing danger, I tried to moderate my opinions. "But he has done some other good things," I said. They looked at me dully.

"You could get drafted, and then you'd have to go to Vietnam," Yarak said.

"I'm only fifteen, so I don't have to make that decision yet," I said.

They listened without curiosity, as though any answer I could have given them would have been negligible or wrong.

"Mohammed and I discussed this, and we think you're a hippie. Hippies don't belong at the same school as us. We think you should get your hair cut too. Didn't President Nixon tell Americans to get haircuts? Where Mohammed and I live disobedience is treason," Yarak said.

"Nixon didn't say that, but maybe you're thinking of Lady Bird Johnson. She said 'Keep America beautiful. Get a haircut' a few years ago. I was going to get one when I went home for Christmas," I said to placate them.

"Well, we don't think you should wait so long. We can give you a haircut tonight. Christmas vacation is almost a month away."

"I'd prefer to wait until I get back to New York, but I promise you both that I will do it. *Je vous jure*," I added. "I swear it to you."

"Well, Mohammed and I think it is too long and we'd like to cut it for you now," he said.

In my head I raced through my escape options: my room maybe, but they'd probably catch me before I made it up the stairs. Down to Café de la Rose? Too far. Maybe my reaction should be more casual, as if I really didn't believe that they were going to scalp me. "Nice talking to you, Yarak," I said as nonchalantly as I could, and walked out through the dining room doors. Before I had time to wonder if they were going to follow me, I was flanked. When I made a move to break away, they grabbed me by the arms and frog-marched me to their room in an outer building, which had a back porch facing away from the courtyard. Mohammed pushed me into a chair on the porch, while Yarak disappeared. He returned a minute later with rope and scissors. Mohammed held my arms behind me, while Yarak wound the rope around me and tied it behind my back. I was petrified. What sort of student kept a spare length of rope in his room?

"I don't have a lot of experience as a barber, but your hair won't mind. You can fix it later if it's crooked," Yarak said. Mohammed giggled. Starting in the front, he cut off the fringe that fell over my eyes, then went to the top of my head before cutting off the long strands at the back that spilled over my shirt collar. Big clumps of hair covered the porch's wooden boards, and what was left on my head felt lopsided. As Yarak cut, he made little clucking noises of self-approval, as if he were repairing the world at the same time that he was shearing me.

"What do you think, Mohammed? Are we done with the little traitor?" Yarak asked.

"Maybe a little more on the sides," he answered.

"*Non*, he's done. Untie him," Yarak commanded.

As soon as I felt the ropes loosen and I could pull my arms free, I took off at a full gallop like a colt. My heart was racing from fear and outrage. I wanted to kill them. I wanted to tie them to chairs and scalp them until they were bald and bloody. I could feel the adrenaline surging in my body and pounding behind my eyes. To calm myself down I leaned against the wall of the main building out of sight, hidden behind a shrub.

This was as much an invasion of my body as the McEnery incident, and made Dad and Ingrid seem civilized by comparison. It puzzled me why so many people were interested in altering me. Even Eric's probing questions about my tryst with Ingrid were invasive. It felt like there was nothing left of me; even my inner resilience, which I had been growing increasingly aware of, had deserted me. Everyone had a clearer vision of my body than I did. It didn't feel as if my body was really mine.

Despairing, doubting my physical existence, I walked jerkily up to my room. I didn't even want to see how they had butchered my hair. I didn't care. I stumbled onto the second-floor landing and heard a few notes of a familiar song: "Lucky Man" by Emerson, Lake and Palmer. Even from the floor below I could hear the chorus: "Ooh, what a lucky man he was."

As I approached my door, I realized that the song was coming from my room. The door was ajar. Pushing it open carefully, I saw a short man swaying to the slow-rising chorus. He was wearing a long blue coat I recognized immediately. When he turned around, I recognized him. He was one of the strange, misshapen men from the asylum. How had he gotten into my room?

I tensed for a confrontation, but as he turned toward me, his chin moist with spit, his eyes bulging under the heavy shelf of his forehead, I could tell by the look in his forlorn eyes that he was harmless. To explain his presence he said quietly and simply, "J'aime la musique qui secoue" (I like the music that shakes). He picked up the needle and put it back to the beginning of the song.

His body, moved by the melody of the chorus, swayed forward and back. I stood next to him. His pleasure seemed genuine and deep. There was no menace in him, even though his hands were balled into fists at his sides. He hummed along, lifted out of himself.

After the song ended, he picked up the needle and put it back to the beginning for a third time. I didn't move to stop him. We listened to it together silently. When it finished I could tell he was going to play it again, but I took the phonograph arm out of his hand as gently as I could and put it back in its cradle. "Il faut rentrer maintenant," I said. (It's time to go back now.) He looked at me with his dark drowsy eyes and slunk toward the staircase.

I felt strangely calm. The intruder left me as peaceful as I had been in months. His serenity lodged in me. I lay on the bed and closed my eyes for a minute before I put the needle back to the beginning of the song. "Ooh, what a lucky man he was," the chorus repeated.

# chapter 9

As soon as I walked in the front door of my house, it was as if the cuckoo clock that we had bought on our first trip to Lausanne and that had stopped the moment I'd left had come unstuck, the plastic figures resuming their regular chores, collecting firewood and circling the snow-draped chalet roof. My brothers and sister sprang to hug me, hanging off my arms and shoulders and clutching my legs, as Sinbad nuzzled his way in, drool hanging from the side of his mouth.

My mother hugged me and then held me at arm's length to take in the whole of me.

I was the same and not the same. Although I had been attacked and hurt, I had expanded, and I could feel that expansion in myself. My confidence had increased, and my French was strong enough to understand most of what was being said in class. Even the slang that was the second language at Café de la Rose, after English, had become part of my vocabulary. I felt bigger, if only in my own eyes. Dad stood a little apart from the others, letting them have the first chance at me.

"What happened to your hair?" Mom asked. My coif at the hands of the Turks had grown out, and I looked like a cross between a small-headed Frankenstein and Rasputin (or some other insane Russian monk); the fringe jagged across my forehead like the teeth of pinking shears, the sides wildly uneven.

"That's a long story," I answered her. "I'll tell you later." Dad came closer and looked at me with his gimlet eye.

"You didn't join that Orthodox church, did you?"

We laughed. Dad's cockeyed humor was pleasantly familiar, as much a part of the house as the curtains and carpet. And the Turkish haircut did have an aspect of messianic lopsidedness.

"I can tell something has changed about you, Jon. It's something in your eyes. They look stronger," Dad said with blithe encouragement.

Tim stood on the stairs behind the group of pets, siblings, and parents. He motioned me to follow him upstairs. When I walked into our bedroom, where everything was exactly the same: the striped bedcovers and bolsters where we tucked our pillows, the orange rug and black easy chair. The poster announcing Jimi Hendrix playing at the Fillmore West in San Francisco was still on the ceiling, as was the one with the Native American with one feather in his headband saying that you didn't have to be Jewish to love Levy's real Jewish rye. The room was a pastoral landscape that I wanted to fit back into as we settled into our beanbag chairs.

"So, what really happened?" Tim asked, staring at my hair.

"Do I have to tell you right now?" I asked him.

"Yup," he said, looking at me intently. "I won't tell anybody if you don't want me to," he said.

"A Turk and a Persian tied me to a chair and cut it. You should have seen it afterward. It looked as if I'd been feathered. It was the worst. I hate those fuckers."

"Did you report them?" he asked.

"Are you kidding?" I said. "Who knows what they would have done to me next if I had ratted on them. Not sure I want to tell Mom and Dad the real story, so keep it to yourself. They wouldn't understand. Dad would want a word with the headmaster, and nothing good would come of that."

"You kind of look like Davy Crockett after he takes his coonskin cap off," Tim said, chuckling. "You should leave it that way. It suits you."


Over the next few days we prepared for Christmas according to my mother's version of it. Although she was Jewish, she had renounced all religious belief, Jewish or otherwise, once she had learned about the Holocaust. Instead she made the holiday a pageant of ornamentation. For my father's sake, she kept a silver menorah in the camera closet, but it was rarely used. He had no particular faith in it, but unlike her he thought not having one under his roof—even one that was tucked away and tarnished—would be inauspicious. Some years we lit a candle on the first or last night of Chanukah or spun the dreidl. Other years it stayed as a kind of unsummoned talisman buried under hats and lenses. Compared with the tall fir tree with its scent of the Vermont forest, the menorah lacked warmth and stature.

In the kitchen carrying out Mom's meticulous instructions, we popped popcorn and sewed the kernels together on long strings that we wound through the branches between the red and green bulbs and the old decorations that we had made in our elementary school arts-and-crafts class. As I hung these childlike ornaments on the tree and wove the popcorn strands through the branches, the bizarre experiences of the last three months faded as the innocence of the embellishments worked their magic.

Mom came and sat down next to me. "Tell me what it's like to be home. It must be a little shocking. Omaha never felt the same after I went away to college. I still loved it, but it felt small and cozy. Way too cozy, almost claustrophobic," she said. I nodded.

"It doesn't feel small here," I said. She reached for my hand and held it between hers. I left it there for as long as I could bear.

"Was it hard?" she asked.

"Yes, very," I said, wanting to avoid details while seeking her sympathy.

"Ellen called me a few days ago before you came home. She said you hadn't been back to stay with them. Any reason?"

"No, not really. I just thought I should make my own friends, not hang around Eric. I don't think he likes me very much," I said.

"Oh, I doubt that. He's probably just caught up in his own activities. I wouldn't worry, Jon. Ellen said that she thought you and Eric were getting on so well," she said. Whether this rosy account came from her maternal optimism or Ellen's, it baffled me.

Sitting next to her, I grew comfortable. I forgot about her intrusions and the secret I had to remember to keep. She made me want to collapse into our past ease, confess everything, so that I could feel casual with her again, forgive and be forgiven. But I knew that there was no realistic chance of that. The wedge that had been driven into our relationship was permanent. Even the idea of her speaking to Ellen about me reminded me of the humiliation of my mistake with Eric and his subsequent betrayal. My naïveté gnawed at me.

"Ellen said you didn't finish what was on your plate and Nathan ate it," she said, smiling, more to recognize my old habits than to chastise me. "She didn't seem to mind. With Nathan a little food more or less wouldn't matter. But you should try to finish what's on your plate." It was rare to hear this urging in my mother's softer voice. It was my father's more insistent command that usually echoed in my head.

"They gave me so much, I could never eat all of it. Nathan took some and then gave the rest to Wolfy," I said, knowing that she thought feeding pets from the dinner table was sinful. She offered no new condemnation. She rose from the sofa and walked toward the kitchen. I knew that I wanted to leave Switzerland behind for the two weeks I would be home. All of it.

We woke up early on Christmas morning and tore open our presents as we always had. The scent of the tree and the stickiness of the sap on our fingers as we reached in to fish more presents out was as intoxicating as it had been when I was little. The early light fell somewhere between the windowpanes and the cushions on the sofa covered in a swirling blue-and-white pattern.


The long drive to northern Vermont for our annual ski trip began the next morning, the giant station wagon overstuffed with gear and bodies. Tim and I sat in the rear seat facing backwards at the unspooling road. "Do you want to learn some dirty French?" I whispered when I grew bored with my book. He nodded eagerly.

"Okay, do you know what a fuck is?" I asked.

"No, what is it?"

"It's a seal," I said.

"Are you sure? How do you spell it?" he asked.

"P-h-o-q-u-e," I answered.

"Who taught you that?" he asked.

"Everybody knows what a seal is," I said.

"Any more?" he asked.

"Yes, one more. Queer in French means 'leather,'" I said.

"It does?" he asked. "What a great language! Is that all?" he asked.

"All for now," I said.

When we couldn't amuse ourselves any more with French homonyms, we started making fun of Cousin Brucie on WABC as he played the year's biggest hits over and over. Tommy James and the Shondells' "Crimson and Clover" and "Crystal Blue Persuasion" were on continuous repeat. We riffed on the lyrics, mangling them and making up our own idiotic versions, tickled with ourselves. We mimicked Brucie's nonstop self-promotion with glee. The two songs became so embedded in my brain that I hummed them to myself unconsciously. Even on the slopes, as I lagged behind my brothers, trying to keep up with their greater speed and appetite for skiing, the songs continued to play in my head.

At least once each trip I would ride up on the chairlift alone with Mom, who was always cold, bundled in more layers than anyone. It snowed when we went together, and we shared the thrill of the slanted white mesh cutting across the mountain. Pointing at the fir trees passing below us, she exclaimed how beautiful snow was, how simple, and sighed. She stuck her black leather mitten out to catch some flakes before they melted. When two of them stuck next to each other on her glove, we stared at them together. "You see how different they are?" she asked. "Each one is unique," she said, "like love. Yours won't be like ours. Yours will be yours. Maybe they should be called loveflakes or snowprints?" she asked in a serious tone. I stared at her glove as the crystals turned into tiny points of water.

Compared with my brothers, I was an unmotivated skier. My mind wandered. I lost interest easily and lagged behind. When I fell near the trees, I sat looking up at the fir branches bending with snow, or searched for voles poking their heads up through the crust. Sometimes I stayed down just to take a break from the nonstop laps on the slope, my brothers always shouting at me to hurry up.

The next day was so cold and clear that the snow, the mountain, and the sky came into sharpened focus. I took the T-bar up the hill, barely managing to hang on as the wooden bar rode up my back. The slope next to the lift was a steep bump run called UN that had frozen solid the night before. The ice, blue like a bruise, made it lethal. Distracted by the cold and birds overhead, I crossed my ski tips and fell, sprawling downhill. My bindings failed to release, and my right leg twisted. A *thwack* went through the thin, frigid air, and I screamed.

I was joined by Tim, and then the ski patrol, and eventually brought down in a sled. When my parents met me in the first aid shelter, my mother burst into tears and hugged me. I felt sorry for myself and brave at the same time. When the pain was bad, it was as if some evil force was ripping my foot away from my knee and then it would subside. After the X-rays were taken, the doctor came in and confirmed what the ski patrol had said: my leg was broken. "You're going to need a full leg cast for three months. And to not put any weight on it. After that it can be cut down to below the knee and you can walk on it," he said.

"Can he fly with it?" Mom asked.

"Oh sure. We make good casts here," he said, smiling at her flirtatiously. After they wound the sheets of dripping wet cloth and plaster, they left a slot at the bottom for my toes to stick out. The cast didn't take long to harden. "Here are your crutches. You walk like this," the doctor said, showing me how to hold the broken leg in front of me.

The nurse gave me painkillers, but they didn't do any good when the throbbing intensified. By the evening, I was in agony. I wasn't hungry and sat through dinner with my cast propped on a pillow. Mom helped me into bed and asked what she could do to make me comfortable. I didn't know. I tried different positions, but sleeping on my back was unnatural and sleeping on my stomach was impossible. I turned from side to side as if I were a rabbit roasting on a spit. Finally, my father, hearing my groans, offered me one of the special blue pills he carried in his private medicine stash. "Take this," he said. "Completely legal." My father traveled with what amounted to a portable pharmacy that cured sleeplessness, muscle ache, and nausea.

An hour or two later, still unable to sleep with my leg swelling as the doctor had warned, I called out again. Dad, fuzzy-haired and disheveled in his pajamas and robe, gave me another blue pill. After that one I fell into such a deep sleep that it was as if my consciousness had been smothered under a giant black tarpaulin. When I woke up, I was sprawled in the back of the station wagon stretched over the duffel bags in the middle section. My mouth was dry and my head was throbbing at a different rate than my pulsing leg. I looked down at the solid white casing and saw my mother's handwriting in black at the top of it, under a bouquet of daffodils. She had been the first to sign it. The others had followed. I rose my head to speak. "Where are we?" I asked.

"Almost home," Dad said. "You've been asleep for almost twenty-four hours. You didn't even stir when we carried you to the car."

"What did you give me?" I asked him.

"Seconal," Mom answered, disapproving of his liberal use of pills, especially with his children. She held up the green-and-beige sock she was knitting to cover my toes, as my foot wouldn't fit inside my regular ones.

Over the next few days I practiced on my crutches. I maneuvered down one hallway and wove back through the living room over the large green rug. I crossed linoleum tiles, then switched to carpeting to test my agility on different flooring. I went up and down the stairs in the back hall before getting up the courage to attempt the main staircase. The pain eased off, and I started to feel more confident in my mobility. Even if I banged the cast accidentally, the reverberation wasn't painful. My leg started to itch almost immediately. When I told Tim how badly I wanted to scratch it, he went into the closet and came back with a wire hanger he untwisted.

"This is what the doctor said to do. You snake it down into the cast and twist it. As your leg withers, it will get easier," he said. Tim, maybe because he had been a wrestler or an asthmatic, always understood the body better than I did.

"Withers?" I said.

"Yes, he said it would shrink because you're not using it." I stuck the wire down the inside of the cast and swiveled it around. With perfect precision, its claw relieved the itch.

"Do you want to go back?" Tim asked.

I pondered this and the questions that followed. How would I make it up and down three flights of stairs to my room five times a day? Would being a cripple provoke further aggression from the Turks, or had they already done everything they wanted to me? I imagined limping between the buildings, hobbling up and down the hill to Café de la Rose, struggling with the vocabulary of a broken leg. And yet, even with all the questions I couldn't answer, I knew I couldn't stay home. The transformation that had taken place in me was subtle but permanent, and my boredom with skiing only reinforced what I knew already: the adventure of the new language, my new friends from Café de la Rose, and even the menace of the Turks provided an excitement that home never could.

After dinner Dad sat down next to me. "Jon, I got you a going-away present," he said. I wasn't sure he was serious. He might offer me something from his gag collection—Groucho Marx dangling eyeballs or a whoopee cushion. Reaching under the chair, he pulled out an unwrapped contraption that he called an arm-muscle exerciser with springs loaded into the handholds. "I want you to keep working on your strength exercises in spite of the broken leg. Your shoulders will get stronger from the crutches. That's the silver lining, so this is the moment to really build yourself up, really put some muscle in your arms and shoulders."

Then he leaned closer and said, "Your mother doesn't know this yet, but I'm coming to Paris soon on business and I want you to meet me there. The school will let you go for a long weekend, won't they?"

"They give permission like that all the time, so I don't see why not," I answered.

"Okay," he declared. "I'll write a formal letter. We'll stay at the Georges Cinq and have a great time together. You can have your own room."

I had begun to think of Europe as mine and preferred that my father remain on his own continent. Even though he wasn't coming to the school, Paris was close enough to make his visit feel like more interference. Maybe he won't really come. Maybe it was one of his brags.

When it was time for me to fly back, Mom drove me to the airport. She seemed particularly nervous, turning the steering wheel jerkily, nudging the car from lane to lane in the dark. She didn't say much, giving me the sense that there was something she was struggling to say.

"Your father has been very difficult lately," she admitted finally. "Maybe he has a work problem he's not telling me about, but something is bothering him. He's always putting his hands on me, pawing me when I don't want him to. I ask him to stop, but he doesn't listen." She looked over at me for support. Previously I might have been more sympathetic, but I felt a hardness in me that obstructed my affection. My instinct in the past had always been to listen to her patiently and to empathize with her troubles, even those with Dad, but that closeness between us had been compromised by her own intrusions with me. My empathy was at best inactive. I couldn't summon it back at will and didn't want to.

She watched me from the side of her eyes and I could tell she was trying to fix me in her mind as I looked that night. She seemed frightened for the future—hers, mine, ours. When she hugged me at the departure gate, she held on to me so long that it felt as if she was trying to preserve parts of me that she was losing track of—a time and place, a familiar position, a ritual of patience.

# chapter 10

B ack in the school's gravel courtyard, I remembered arriving for the first time with my parents. The day was bright. The sun enhanced the charm of the odd buildings with their dipping rooflines, and I was filled with some of my original excitement. The other part of me was streaked with the memory of the disturbing events that had occurred out of sight: arms pinning my own and rope tied behind my back. Going up the front steps, I knew I had to get as far away from those incidents as I could.

The taxi driver carried my blue tweed bags up the three flights of stairs to my room. With him huffing behind me, I made it to the top. From the bed, I took an inventory of the belongings I had left behind. The clothes still showed a few signs of the original order Mom had put them in. For a second I felt the emptiness of the room and missed her and home, but then I looked around and was reassured by my stereo and my records and the books sitting on the shelf.

On Sunday evening Serge poked his head in and immediately saw the cast. "What happened to you?"

"I went skiing in Vermont and broke my leg. A three-month sentence in this white palace," I said, tapping on the plaster. "What about you?"

"We went to our chalet in Crans-Montana. André was there with his family too. It was great," he said. Before leaving, he taught me the French for "cast," "crutches," and "limping." Still, I couldn't stand him and André and their smugly entitled friends from Geneva who acted as if their lives and their futures working for their fathers in their private banks were foregone conclusions. The next day at Café de la Rose the reception was more enthusiastic. When Axel saw me hobble toward him, he broke off a piece of Nepalese black and offered it to me free of charge. "You'll need this," he said in his bemused way.

"Axel, how do I find another place to live? I can't take the Turkish warriors or the Geneva crowd anymore. They are a bunch of mercenaries in training."

"Why didn't you say so before? I know just the guy for you. The crazy Greek." Axel put his chubby fingers in his full cheeks and wolf-whistled across the smoky room so piercingly that everyone froze in the middle of their foosball and pinball games. He pointed to a small hairy guy playing at a machine in the corner. "You need the hippie," he said. "His name is John. He is a little strange."

Having been summoned, John pushed his way through the crowd. His frame was small like mine, but it was easy to tell through his clothes that he wasn't a lightweight and therefore in a higher physical category than I was. He sported a standard green Vietnam-style combat jacket over what I came to recognize as his uniform of tight jeans and black clunky shoes.

"Jon is looking for a new room or roommate," Axel said to him. "Any ideas?"

"Yes, you gotta come live in the Annex with us. There's an empty bed in Ibengue's room. I think he's here," John said, swiveling around. "Ibengue!" he shouted. To me he said, "He has the best grass in Lausanne, man. Diplomatic pouch privileges."

"What's that?" I asked.

"His father is the minister of religion in the Congo. He brings in whatever he wants, and customs doesn't have the right to check because his father is in the cabinet." The blackest boy I had ever seen came toward us.

"Who's this?" he asked in a slow, almost lazy French drawl, pointing at me.

"A new kid from New York," John said.

"What happened here?" he asked, pointing at my cast.

"Ski crash," I answered.

"In Kinshasa we don't ski," he said, referring to his hometown in the capital of the Congo. "And only the Communists have broken legs," he said in his languorous accent. "Come with me. I'll show you the room."

We walked back up the hill together toward the Annex. "What do I say to Buehler?" I asked him. I sensed that he knew how to get what he needed from the administration better than I did.

"You're limping. You have a cast up to your shorts. You can't go up and down those stairs seven times a day. It's impossible," he said. In the Annex there were only two floors with five kids on each. The room Ibengue and I would share was large and had a door to a balcony.

"Good thinking," I said.

"Look at this landscape!" he said, pointing to the view from outside. We could see the reddish roofs of the town and Lake Geneva far below us. It was almost as good a view of the lake as the one from the Mitnicks' house. To the right, I could see the forecourt of the asylum beyond other walls and buildings.

"Formidable!" I said.

"Go talk to Buehler now before he sends me a Turkish psychopath," he said.

Buehler greeted me in his doorway. Before I could say a word he asked: "Room change?"

"Yes, with the leg in a cast I can't handle the stairs," I said.

"Room with Ibengue then?" he asked. I nodded. "Attention," he said, urging caution. "The asylum is next door."

With a wheelbarrow borrowed from the maintenance shed I carted all my belongings that didn't fit in the fraying blue suitcases. When I poked open the door of my new room with the tip of my crutch, a cascade of water landed on my head and dripped down my jacket. I was stunned and looked up at Ibengue, who was grinning as he leaned against the windowsill.

"Velcome, Vells!" he said, smiling, sounding not unlike my Yiddish-speaking paternal grandmother. "I love that trick," he said. "I hope your cast didn't melt!"

After drying off and setting up my stereo, I wandered next door to peer into John's room. He was standing in front of an easel with a red painting on it, his feet set wide apart. It was a scene of smallish white orbs against a splotchy red background, perhaps satellites or planets, whirling through space. From the giant headphones that gave his hive of curly hair a deranged shape I could hear Janis Joplin singing, "C'mon now, baby," as he daubed more paint onto the canvas between the white discs. I left before he spotted me and returned to Ibengue, who was rolling a joint with marijuana that he'd pulled from a green pouch.

"Where did that come from?" I asked, wanting to get the story directly.

"My country," he said. I hadn't seen grass since I'd been in Switzerland, although I had seen hash in every shade of brown and black and from gooey to hard in composition. Grass didn't come from hash countries, I had learned.

"Nobody else has that," I said.

Ibengue explained that his father was the minister of religion for Mobutu, president of the Congo, and that it was a horrible job but had its benefits. *"Fraîche!"* he said, sticking his nose in. "The scent reminds me of home," he said. The grass in his pouch was aromatic and sticky. The resin webbed my fingers. Ibengue rolled a perfect joint and, as I discovered later, he could even roll them in the dark and they'd turn out aerodynamically slim and tapered.

After a few tokes, he suggested I introduce myself to François, a French boy from Marseilles who lived down the hall. Since I was high, that seemed like as good an idea as any, so I limped along the hall and knocked on the door. He let me in and asked, "Are you Ibengue's new roommate? What happened to you?" I already felt fluent in the vocabulary of my predicament.

*"Tant pis,"* he said, using the perfect phrase of lament for my situation. "If that happened to me, my parents wouldn't let me come back to school because I couldn't make the trip. I go home almost every weekend," he said.

"Why's that?" I asked him.

"I miss my family," he said.

"You're lucky you can go home so easily," I said.

Later that evening I recounted the conversation to Ibengue. He listened for a few minutes with a serious face and then burst out laughing. "What a bullshitter," he said. "He hates his family. And they hate him too. Coming and going is his job. He's a mule," he explained. He continued in English: "Yes, that's his job. His family owns one of the biggest garages in Marseilles, and he brings the cash back to deposit in the bank on Monday afternoon. Don't ever walk in on him without knocking. Especially Sunday night. I did it once while he was getting undressed. I couldn't believe it."

"What do you mean?" I asked.

"His body was full of francs. He had thousands of notes strapped to his body. He had money in his underwear, his socks, his T-shirt. He was a shrub of money. They were everywhere. His parents pay the tuition but he's not really a student like we are. He's really a smuggler, and the school is just a façade," he said.

The subject matter went way beyond the little common sense I had. I needed to think it through step by step—François was a mule for the family business? "Why?" I asked him.

"To avoid the high taxes in France. The cash he smuggles the French tax authorities can't find. His father is a tax expert, or tax avoider I should say, and makes him do it. If not, it's no school and learning to be a car mechanic. We're all smugglers here one way or the other. I am. What about you?" he asked me.

"I'm not smuggling anything. My parents just sent me here because they thought it was safer and I'd learn French," I answered.

"Nobody here would believe that story, so let's just say, *entre nous,* that you're going to smuggle French back into America," he said with one of his broad smiles that made me feel like a coconspirator.

"What about you?" I asked him.

"Grass, as you have already noticed," he said. "And other things, too, for my father, but let's talk about that another time."

"Well, what about John? Is he a smuggler?"

"No, he's more like me. A political refugee. His father is under house arrest in Athens. Has been for years. When the Greek colonels with the help of the CIA and the US Navy helped stage their coup and took over the country, his father was one of the opposition leaders. He decided it was time for John to get out even if he couldn't, and maybe he thought that if John was abroad, the colonels might let him leave for an occasional visit. And it looks better in the press if they allow the son to flee." He must have thought I was an idiot. My mouth hung open. This was the wildest bunch of kids I had ever met.

"What about your father?" I asked him, unable to contain my curiosity. "Is he why you're here too?"

"Kind of. Mobutu, our president, is a despot. And paranoiac. He kills whoever he thinks is against him. He has many enemies. Lumumba. The Communists in Brazzaville, the capital of the country next to ours, the Republic of Congo. Now he thinks the world is against him, so he's gone crazy. And he's a thief stealing money that was meant for our people. He stole ten billion dollars of American aid, some say. To make people afraid, he started holding public hangings in the Kinshasa soccer stadium every Saturday. My father, because he's the religion minister, has to give the victims last rites, and our family is forced to attend and watch. I couldn't take the hangings anymore, and that's how I wound up here. I never want to hear the sound of a neck breaking again," he said, and stared at the floor. A moment later he looked back up, the broad smile affixed to his face. "Of course, no benefits make up for such crimes," he said.

When Ibengue left the room, I took my Dylan Thomas *Collected Poems* down from the shelf. I needed to hold on to something to anchor me. Ibengue's stories were so outlandish, it was hard to believe they were true, and yet there were too many details for them to be invented. Next to my new friends, my hard-won maturity and independence were laughable. Their world of smuggling money and drugs and political executions went far beyond my trivial suburban trauma. What I thought was harrowing would probably make them laugh. Next to them I was a naïf who understood nothing about the broader world. Ibengue's stories made me wonder about Axel and the others at Café de la Rose. What were they really doing at the

École Nouvelle, and why were they calling themselves exiles and laughing at the word among themselves? Were they smugglers too?

Out of curiosity, more than anything else, I found myself visiting John as I settled in at the Annex. John never spoke of his father's house arrest. Nor did he ever refer to much about his home or his family. There were no photographs of them in his room or knick-knacks to remind him of them. There were easels, cans of paint, and drop cloths. The air reeked of turpentine. On his shelves he kept a few paperbacks in English, such as *The Doors of Perception* by Aldous Huxley and *Siddhartha* by Hermann Hesse, which looked as if they had been read so many times, the pages might fall out if the books were taken off the shelves. When it came to talking about his books and what he learned from them, John was intense, dogmatic, and humorless. That was what I found fascinating about him.

Most often our conversations began as discussions and ended as arguments. He would make a statement such as, "LSD is the only way to navigate the world. It should be available by prescription. There's a drug for everything else, so why not for perception?" It was hard for me not to be drawn into taking the opposite side of the argument because his views were so intractable. If I said, "Not everyone wants to have their mind altered by a drug, John. Some people find the world fascinating as it is," he'd say, "How do you know? Have you ever taken it?"

"No, I've never tried it," I admitted.

After weeks of debate, John wore me down. That Saturday night we ate the blotter paper together and then walked out into the fresh spring evening. We passed the shuttered Café de la Rose and wandered toward the pine forest in the hills near the Mitnicks' house. I didn't feel anything initially, and then the next moment the amphetamines in the LSD overwhelmed me. Suddenly, it was as if I had been captured by paramilitary soldiers and force-marched toward the forest. They took hold of my padded jacket with a grip as heavy as the Turks', yanking me along the streets as fast as I could go with my crutches and cast.

"John, what's happening? This is awful. How long will it last?" I asked him, starting to panic.

"That's the speedy part of the trip," John said, as if naming it would make it ease off. "Stay cool, man. It doesn't last long."

"Then what happens?" I asked.

"You'll see stuff, incredible stuff," he answered.

"Is the pavement moving?" I asked him when we sat down on a bench under a streetlamp.

"No, it's flat, but I see what you mean. It's got diamonds in it, right?"

Before I could separate the glittering stones, a Swiss gendarme walked toward us. "Good evening, gentlemen. What are you doing here?" he asked us in the typical singsong accent of the area, loitering in that district of elegant homes at two o'clock in the morning. He seemed more lonely than suspicious. "May I see your identity cards?" he asked as a formality. We handed over our student cards casually. John was calm, not combative, speaking in his clearest French, without the lisp that sometimes hampered him. He conversed with the officer as if it were a balmy afternoon and we were about to unpack a picnic hamper, while I watched the policeman's face turn from human skin into the iridescent scales of a fish struggling upstream.

"You boys weren't in the university demonstrations today by any chance?" he asked us.

"*Non,*" we both said as he asked about the protests that had taken place that day in Lausanne and spread to all the universities in Switzerland. "They were peaceful at least, but even so," he said. "This isn't Swiss, this. Maybe in America they can do this kind of thing. Or Paris. But we are Swiss," he said, as if that simple assertion explained everything that was wrong with them. "Maybe it's time to go back to your school?" he suggested without ordering us. We took his advice and headed back toward École Nouvelle. The pavement still swayed under my crutches as I tried to manage the undulations. John was rapturous.

"Did you see his face, man?" he asked me, nearly howling with excitement. "It turned into an old-fashioned streetlamp. His nose was a wick, and the flame in each eye turned blue and danced around. You didn't talk much," he added.

"I forgot most of my French. His face turned into the tail of a trout," I said.

"Cool," John said.

Falling asleep at dawn, I slept into the late afternoon. When I woke up the room felt dingy. Ibengue was gone. I had a bitter taste in my mouth that I couldn't spit out. The policeman's face reappeared, shimmering and writhing. The ground felt like a roller coaster. I would have given anything for the flashbacks to stop. Even a long shower didn't rinse out the drug's residue. When Ibengue came back from lunch hours later, I was still sitting on my bed in a stupor.

"Where were you and John last night?" he asked. "Did you take some of his voodoo powder? No, please no. I hope not. You can see how much good it's done him. Take it again and you'll end up like him, painting outer space." Until Ibengue mentioned that, it hadn't occurred to me that John's paintings were hallucinations that he was trying to capture.

"I took a shower. What else can I do to get rid of the feeling?" I asked him.

"I don't know, my friend," he said. "Take another one. And this time make it cold!" I took my towel and limped back to the bathroom, my cast wrapped in the plastic sleeve I had fashioned for it, sealed with an elastic band at the top. I made the water as cold as I could tolerate. The shock of it jolted me but didn't clear the cobwebs. When I got out I looked at my face in the mirror. It was as tired as it had ever looked. My eyes were bloodshot, and the skin sagged under them.

On the way back to my room I ran into Marco, one of the two Swiss Italians who lived downstairs. He was a smuggler too, according to Ibengue, except he smuggled Italian lire from Italy into Lugano, Switzerland, where he lived. He was tall and stringy with freckles on his face; Ray-Ban aviator sunglasses were always hooked over the top button of his gaping shirt, and the loose gold bracelet he wore made an expensive, annoying noise. His state was one of preternatural calm, as if at any moment a customs officer might search his bags and he had to pose as an innocent, an ordinary student. He asked what Ibengue and I were doing that night, and then, without warning, he lurched toward me and kissed me on the lips before I had a chance to pull away from him. The foul aroma of his cologne assaulted me.

"What are you fucking doing?" I shouted, staring at his pouty, unshaven cheeks as he nervously shook his bracelet. He didn't blink, and inched his face closer to me again. This time I pushed him back. That made him slink away toward the stairs.

I felt a seething anger rise in me. I wanted to run after him, spin him around, and punch him in the face, but I stood rooted to the spot. I was paralyzed. My immobility made me furious at myself rather than him. Why hadn't I punched him or hit him with my crutch? Why had I held myself back? Why was I still standing there? I tried to calm myself down and block out the fury that I felt as if I had no right to it. My method for coping with Marco's assault was pure denial. It meant nothing. It had nothing to do with Dad's doubts about my manliness. Marco's act proved nothing. After these recitals, I felt a surge of energy but I had no strength in my legs or shoulders, so I slouched back to my bed with the resentment and offense burning inside me.

As I lay there searching the ceiling, I realized that this was my first real kiss. Ingrid had brushed my cheek with her lips, but she hadn't kissed mine. The fact that it was sprung on me against my will by a boy only increased its weirdness and sadness. I could still feel his beard scraping against my chin as if a lizard had swiped my face with its scaly tail. He repulsed me. I loathed the sight of him. It proved that Dad was completely wrong, didn't it? I wasn't queer. I never wanted to feel rough stubble on my cheek again.

That night I wrote my father a letter, not mentioning what Marco had done but confessing to the LSD trip. I reasoned that if I told him about it, I could exonerate myself and he would forgive me. I wrote the details down on onionskin paper with my new fountain pen. As soon as I was done, I sealed it and put a stamp on it and stuck it in the letterbox so I couldn't change my mind. It was only after I mailed it that I began to wonder if I wanted to shock him with the news as much as be forgiven. Why would I want to shock him? Maybe it was to make him think that he had underestimated me and this act of defiance would announce who I really was. But my hunch was that if I had told him what had really happened with Marco, he would have asked, What were you doing all those push-ups for if it wasn't to sock this guy in the jaw?

When Ibengue came back to the room that night and I confided in him about what Marco had done, he asked me, "Are you surprised? What did you expect from that freak? That guy's weird. I always thought so. It makes me wonder what happened to his last roommate. Who'd want to move in with him? Or maybe he just likes American boys?" He smirked, not expecting an answer.

The next day I felt almost normal again. The policeman's face came and went in a flash while I was trying to understand Rabelais and Gargantua. Marco's beard scratched against my cheek again, distracting me from the difficult archaic French. Even though the two events weren't related, they became intertwined. Other fragments of that night and the next day swam back into focus and faded again almost as quickly.

On the Monday afternoon after class, John came in and sat down on Ibengue's bed. "Are you having flashbacks too?" I asked him.

"Yes, but they don't bother me," John said. "I kind of like them. They bring back everything I learned."

"What did you learn? I didn't learn anything except that we were lucky not to get arrested. Other than that, there were a bunch of hallucinations that didn't add up to much," I said.

"I learned it wasn't serious. None of it was. Not the policeman or the demonstrations. Not even the drug. Let's take it again next weekend," he said.

"I don't want to take it again, John. I wrote my father and told him I did it," I said.

"Why did you do that? You couldn't live with it? You had to confess? Who else did you tell?" he asked me.

"Just Ibengue," I said.

"That's fine. He knows anyway. I can't believe you told your father. What if he tells the school?" he asked.

"He won't. I'm sure he won't make an issue of my taking it but I don't want to take it again," I answered.

"Why not?" he asked.

"I hated the speed and how long the hallucinations lasted. It was too heavy for me," I said.

"So you believe in only one reality, then?" he asked, as if we were having a philosophical debate.

"No, there are different realities, but I like my senses as they are, not turned up to maximum volume," I said.

"You've got it all wrong, man. Those experiences are all one frequency," he said. "You need LSD to get to the others."

"Well, I guess I'll have to live without them," I said.

Our different perspectives widened into a philosophical breach that grew bigger over the next few days. John saw my point of view as a repudiation of his beliefs and reacted with hurt surprise, a feeling of betrayal. Within a few days he stopped speaking to me, barely saying hello as he passed me in the hallway. I became a ghost.

Soon I noticed that François was not speaking to me either. "What did I do to you?" I asked him.

"Not much, but I agree with John, and when you go to the bathroom in the middle of the night you make a loud thumping noise. The heel of the cast bumps on the floor like a dead man knocking on my door. It gives me nightmares, and I wake up sweating." I looked at him, thinking he might only be teasing me, but his face didn't break a smile. "How could such a small guy who weighs next to nothing make so much noise? I ask myself. How much *do* you weigh?"

"I don't know. I haven't weighed myself in a while," I answered.

"Probably not even fifty kilos I bet. Since you are so light, I realized it must be how you walk that makes you loud. Then it came to me. You walk on your heels. Did you know that?" he asked. The French word for "heel," *talon*, was new to me.

"No, I had no idea," I said. "It must be the cast."

"Yes, it must be the cast. It couldn't be you," he said mockingly. "Because without the cast you don't weigh enough to sink a dog."

"What does that mean?" I asked.

"Think about it," he said, and walked off. But of course it didn't matter what its literal meaning was—it was an insult of lightweightedness, my first one in a long time.

Once John and François stopped speaking to me, they convinced the others, except Ibengue, to stop too. John was the ringleader. He argued that my position on LSD was the symptom of a bigger flaw, and by rejecting the drug I was rejecting them as a group. The reason I was doing that, according to him, was that underneath the long hair and flowery shirts I wore, I was soft and ordinary. And a square. Evidence of that lowly condition was the letter I wrote my father about taking LSD. Only a bourgeois kid from a stable family would be so obsequious. The letter was proof that I was still a child and unmanly, a critique that echoed some of my father's. His parents are married, John said to them about my family. They are happy and still living together in their big suburban house. He has three younger siblings he corresponds with, and they have two dogs and a cat. He is a perfect example of the normal bourgeois American teenager. His home is so conventional, Ibengue reported him saying, that he belongs on a television sitcom as a perfect example of American life. For John, this was as reactionary, uncool, and revolting as a human being could be. If I tried to refute the one-sided picture he painted, he simply walked away.

He was partly right. Compared with the group in the Annex, I was conventional. I wasn't used as a mule by my family to smuggle money into Switzerland. I didn't bear witness to the crimes of heads of state. And yet, Ibengue and even John had asked me so many questions about my home and family that I suspected they were envious of its apparent tranquility. My life was as exotic to them as theirs were to me.

The silent treatment lasted a week and might have lasted longer had it not been interrupted by my trip to Paris to meet my father. The day before I left I received a rare, undictated, handwritten letter back from him. He forgave my drug taking and glossed over the experience as if it wasn't particularly remarkable. Everything should be tried once, he wrote. Experimentation was no foundation for shame.

# chapter 11

My father opened the door to his room at the Hotel George V and looked as fresh as if he had just awakened from a full night's sleep even though he had only arrived that morning from New York. His tan suit was uncreased. The brown checked tie was still cinched against his throat. His black hair shone. Quickly, he gave me a hug and pointed to the receiver lying on the desk. He motioned me to sit down and returned to his business call. I was used to him making me wait, so I sat down on the puffy sofa and hoisted my cast up to the marble coffee table. The room was plush. Curtains with multicolor tassels hung above the windows. The walls were padded and wrapped in silk. Dad continued his conversation in a leisurely, long-winded manner. After the silent treatment I'd been receiving at school, his gruff, monosyllabic voice was reassuring.

When he finally hung up, he looked at me and my cast. He came over and gave it a knock with his knuckle. "Holding up I see. How are your shoulders doing?" he asked. He placed a hand on each one and gave them a squeeze. I suddenly remembered the exerciser he had given me that had been abandoned somewhere, unused, when I switched rooms. "Did the crutches help? Let me see. Flex," he commanded. I gave him a look asking if I really had to. The answer in his brown eyes was clear. I flexed. "A distinct improvement," he said. "But there's more work to be done. Look, I'm pretty busy in meetings most of the day, but we can have dinner together every night. Here's some money. Enjoy yourself."

I walked the Paris streets on my crutches for as long as I could stand. I went to the Louvre and back to l'Orangerie to see Monet's *Water Lilies*. With Dad's money I bought a green crushed-velvet suit and green stack-heel leather boots from a store on the place de la Madeleine. I felt liberated from Lausanne, my dorm room in the Annex, and the shame and isolation of my friends' treatment.

Dinner conversation with Dad was the usual mixture of exhortation and reminiscence. "You have no idea how rough the Depression was. My father didn't have a law practice for ten years. We only had a place to live thanks to a former client who had a spare apartment. And that was after we had snuck out of two places in the middle of the night because my father couldn't pay the rent. I remember holding my shoes in my hands so I wouldn't make any noise on the stairs. I was nine or ten. It made us tough and hungry watching my father play pinochle every day for a decade. That's why it is so important for you to build your body, broaden yourself. I want you to be a man of substance, not air, not a luftmensch like my father's friends were. They never went back to work. They got thinner and thinner. In the old days, luftmentschen floated from town to town. They had no ballast. They told stories. They entertained. Without gainful employment. No regular meals. I don't want you to be one of them. That's my point to you."

On the day before my return to school he announced that he couldn't have dinner with me that night because he had to meet with a business associate but suggested that we have a drink together in the hotel bar instead. It was Saturday night. I put on my new green suit, the right pant leg ripped to the thigh to accommodate the cast, my new paisley shirt, and one boot. Riding down in the elevator with its gilded arrows and laurel leaves, I looked in the mirror and felt cautiously confident of my strength and stability. I felt almost prepared to go back to school the next day to face my former friends.

Dad ordered a vodka and tonic for himself and a Coke for me. "What are you going to do tonight? Would you like some company?" he asked me. I didn't understand what he meant. He turned sideways to look at the three women who were sitting in a row at the bar. "How about one of them," he said. "Couldn't do you any harm. Which one would you like?" he asked. He tapped the heavy brass room key on the marble table and in unison the trio pivoted their brittle hairdos. "You choose, or shall I choose for you?"

Because I felt as if I had no choice, I fixed my eyes on the dark-haired woman on the right. The kohl liner around her eyes and her olive skin felt like the challenge of the unknown or the inarticulate or both. She resembled Claudia Cardinale, curvy and ample. Dad gestured to her theatrically, and she walked over to us. He pointed at me to make it clear that he wasn't the customer, only the financier. "Show her your room key so she can see the number," he said to me. She nodded as if no other explanation was necessary. Gesturing at his watch and holding up all ten fingers, he directed her attention to my cast to convey how long it would take me to get back to the room.

For a second I thought about rebelling, frozen in my chair and feeling both of them watching me. The web of his ideas and expectations tightened on my body. For a few seconds I didn't know what I would decide until I felt something scratchy on my cheek and remembered the scrape of Marco's beard. Then I stood up immediately, tucked my crutches under my arms, and started moving slowly along the harlequin tiles toward the elevators. I could feel them watching me as I limped down the hall, and I was grateful for the shelter when the elevator doors closed behind me. As I rode up to my floor, I saw again her stuffing the five oversized hundred-franc notes my father gave her into her dimpled leather purse, a brief motherly indulgence passing across her face.

In my room, I put my crutches in the corner and began to think where I should wait for her. The bed was premature. The desk falsely studious. That left the small couch, so I sank into its feathers, nervous and sweaty. When she knocked, I yanked myself up, holding on to the table, and hopped across the carpet to let her in. She carried with her a faint scent of cigarettes and magnolia blossoms. Pausing in front of me, she said, "But you are a child. How old are you?"

"I'm fifteen, mademoiselle," I answered sheepishly.

"Well, you're not much for fifteen, are you?" she remarked, seeming to not believe either my age or my size. She shifted her eyes to my cast. "And how did you do that?" she asked as she led me to the sofa, her arm around my waist, and guided me down next to her. "Is this your first time?" she asked. Anxious and muddled, I wasn't sure whether she was referring to my first broken leg or the first time I had been alone with a woman.

"It is my first time. Yes," I said. She smiled, obviously interpreting my answer as if it was the latter question and the more interesting one.

"Well, this is the first time I have been with a boy whose leg is in a cast, so we are both virgins tonight," she said, and smiled at me. I didn't have the heart to tell her that it was only my first time in a cast.

I asked her questions as if we had just met in a bar. Where are you from? What is your name? I wasn't sure how much I was allowed to know. She said her name was Natalie and she was from the south, gesturing somewhere in the far part of the room near the closets. I imagined Corsica and its palm trees or the south of Spain, where I had never been. Her accent sounded Mediterranean, as if Italian or, more likely, Spanish was her native language. When she answered my questions while looking away from me, I tried to see behind her eyes for any hint of doubt in her, but they were as glittering a shield as the rest of her body—metallically intriguing and seductive. I felt myself pulled toward her and realized how attracted I was to her.

She came closer and folded my head beneath her chin. She kissed my scalp and roughed my hair, which was now longer than it had been before the Turks had cut it. Beneath her perfume I could smell her skin as she held me. It was earthy and aromatic. The filial position with my eyes almost closed under her protection was too emotionally powerful, so I backed away and tried not to search for the spot where she had sheltered me.

She leaned over and kissed me on the lips like Marco had, except her lips were pillowy and soothing. As if I were a little boy, she took my hand and helped me up. She led me to the bed and unbuttoned my shirt. Everything she did felt kind and without external considerations. The first article of clothing she removed was her watch.

Natalie took my pants off cautiously, as if the break in my leg was fresh and still painful. She asked me to unsnap her bra, which I couldn't do, and then did it herself. Her breasts were dark and heavy. They pressed against my side as she lay next to me, her arm across my stomach. When she raised herself on top of me, I watched her look away from me as she rode up and down. When she lifted her body up, I could see the bouquet of flowers my mother had drawn in Magic Marker at the top of my cast. When she lowered herself again, the petals disappeared under her thighs.

If it was even possible, she felt better to me than Ingrid had. She was more imposing and solid. I liked the feeling of her weight on me, as if I could lose myself under her and vanish. I followed her eyes as she looked beyond me, above my head, from side to side. I wanted her to take me with her wherever she was going and not be left behind. I tried to hold myself back from coming, to make the warmth and pleasure last, but I couldn't. She rolled over next to me, looked in my eyes, and kissed the hair on the side of my head like my mother used to do when we were in public. Her kiss was so soft and genuine that I was convinced I was special to her in some way I couldn't imagine.

Natalie didn't rush to put her clothes back on. She lay on her side looking at me. I felt no shame about my skinniness because she had already seen it—and stayed. She placed her hand on the pit of my stomach and pressed her palm into its concavity. No one had ever touched me there, and by doing so she transferred a value to it that it had never had before. She moved the heel of her hand from one side of my stomach to the other and then touched the tips of her fingers along each protruding rib, pretending to play them as if they were the raised black keys on a meager piano. She rested her head on my chest, listening to the choppy music of my heart. Then she tilted her head up, smiled, and said in her smoker's voice, "You are so thin, *mon petit*. You have to eat. It's that simple. What's wrong? You don't like to eat?"

"Everyone is always trying to get me to eat. I'm sick of it. I want to eat when I'm hungry, not when they're hungry," I said, surprised at the words that came out of my mouth; it felt like they had the power of revelation.

"Forget about the others. Eat for me," she said fiercely, as if her devotion to my body would outlast our time together. I felt no shame in her command. For a lingering moment, her indulgent intensity next to me, I wanted to obey her blindly and please her, eat more than ever, stoke my appetite for her.

Without having to look at her watch, she knew when the hour had passed and sat up, scanning the room. Her bra was on the bed, and the rest of her clothes were folded over the arm of the chair next to my resplendent green suit. Her handbag was on the coffee table. I could tell that she was sequencing the stages of her departure, and I didn't want her to go. I wanted to cling to her and her belief in me. If I'd had enough money to keep her with me all night, I would have paid her without another thought. As if she could tell what I was thinking, she leaned over and kissed my forehead lovingly.

She stood up and put her clothes on as methodically as she had removed them. I wondered how many times a night she dressed and undressed, stepping in front of the mirror to make sure she looked her best before leaving. How many boys had felt as encouraged by her as I had? She must know every room in this hotel, I thought to myself. She must know where the mirrors are and the Kleenex boxes and the path to each bathroom and where all the light switches are. While I was imagining her as the queen of the Hotel George V, she came back and sat next to me on the bed. "Come and visit me again. Next time I want to see you a little fuller. You know where to find me now," she said. "But just in case, I wrote my number down. Call me when you return." I looked at the piece of paper. It said, "Natalie— Odeon 49 61." She brushed my stomach with the back of her hand, stood up, and walked out without looking at me again.

The door closed before I could plead for her to stay. As soon as she was gone, I doubted whether she had been there at all and if her encouragement was real. Ingrid hadn't said anything that made me feel better. I tried to bring back Natalie's warmth and compassion, her moving slowly on top of me, anchoring me so I wouldn't float away like a "man of air," but she kept fading. When she had been in my room she seemed like a woman who had always known and loved me. Or could only a stranger make me feel like that? I wondered.

Stretched out on the bed, naked except for the cast ornamented with my friends' and family's signatures and drawings, I was immobilized. My leg ached inside the cast. In spite of the heavy impression her body had made on mine—the sublime inversion of McEnery's cruel weight—I wanted to leap up and peek through the keyhole to see if I could still catch a glimpse of her waiting for the elevator but I didn't move.

With my head on the pillow I started to imagine the food I would eat for her: vats of ice cream, giant coconut pies with vanilla icing, and countless pastries. Then I realized that it was dark and I was starving. I began to assemble the ideal room service dinner in my mind as a tribute to her and her wish that I eat more. I designed the biggest meal I could think of and served it to myself. As an appetizer I would order an avocado. I had eaten my first one in Paris only a few days before, the place where the pit had been filled with a vinaigrette dressing. For my main course, I'd want a steak grilled lattice style with a pat of herb butter that melted into the black grill marks, leaving behind flecks of green. The butter would run onto the plate beneath the mound of golden, slightly crusted French fries. I'd tear off bits of baguette and soak up the herbed butter sauce. I'd spear the fries in bunches with my fork. For dessert I'd order a plate of profiteroles, savoring the ice cream between the doughy pastry. I was ravenous in Natalie's honor. I could finish all of it. She had liberated me from my resistance to food, my protests against my father's criticisms and commands and McEnery and the Mitnicks and all of the other adults who had chided me about my eating deficiencies. She nudged me into the future. In my closed eyes, I reimagined the playing card that I had first seen after Eric had betrayed me. My colors were bright now. My rank was high. I was sure of my powers.

After devouring every morsel of this fantasy meal and licking my imaginary knife, I reached for the remote control and turned on the television set. Johnny Hallyday, the veteran French pop star, filled the screen with his synthetic blond hair and reptilian face, his body too old and stringy to be wearing a studded white jumpsuit. He sang a few verses of his hit song, leaping around the stage with false emotion. I struggled to make out the lyrics and fell asleep before I had a chance to order dinner.

The next morning Dad asked, "How was your date?" I shrugged, not wanting to share any of the Natalie experience with him, not wanting to even pronounce her name in his presence. She was sacred.

"Can I see her again before I go? She gave me her telephone number." I blurted, unable to hide my desire to be in her presence again.

"No, Jon. Forget about her," he said. "You have to go back to school, and I have to go to London. Don't get stuck on her. There are a thousand girls like her. Any taxi driver in any city in the world can lead you to one. Put her out of your mind and go back to Lausanne." I didn't want to hear his desultory comments and tried to block them out. I wanted to cherish the warmth Natalie had left in me.

"She was kind," was all I could mutter in her defense.

"They're all kind, Jon. That's part of the job. I'll find other girls for you when you're back in New York," he said.

At that moment nothing could have interested me less. I thought about all the other women he had told Tim and me about over the years, old girlfriends, random women on the street, all of them merely sport. Chasing them, seducing them, closing the sale, all a game that heightened his selling instincts, that required skill and concentration, agility and persuasion. Any trace of emotion or what I had felt for Natalie was not part of this game.

On the train back to Lausanne, I continued my eating fantasy, inspired by Natalie directions. It wasn't only the command itself that made it powerful. Everyone had ordered me to eat. It was how she invested eating with the pleasure it would give her to see me more filled out, more solid on my feet. It was for my benefit, not hers. She would be an admirer of my progress from a distance, without an agenda of her own. She cared for me, and I wanted to eat to please her.

# chapter 12

I t wasn't until my taxi pulled up to the door of the Annex that I remembered the silent treatment that I had left behind. Paris had completely, if temporarily, erased it. As I lay on my bed again, the hurt of it returned. Maybe my absence would have the same amnesiac effect on my adversaries that it had on me. Aside from disagreeing with John about the value of hallucinogens and my cast bumping on the floor at night, I wasn't sure what I had done to deserve their shunning.

Ibengue walked into the room and said loudly, as if he were preaching, "I am happy to see you again, my son."

"Where are the others?" I asked.

"They'll be back soon," he answered.

"Are they still angry?" I asked.

"Maybe, maybe not, but they're stoned, so it may not matter too much. They are macaques," he added, comparing them to the monkeys who lived in his Kinshasa backyard, the image he always used to describe imbecility. That I felt less threatened by them might have had something to do with Natalie. Their influence had waned.

One by one, John, François, and Marco shuffled into the room. Axel, who wasn't often there on the weekends, appeared too. They moved around aimlessly, seeming uncomfortable with my reappearance. "So where have you been?" Axel asked.

"Paris with my father. He was there on a business trip, so I went to meet him."

"Oh," Axel responded. They all looked at me as if to say, Is that all you can tell us? I saw Marco staring at me and I wanted to neutralize him most of all.

"What did you do there?" John said, his prodding giving me the opening.

"Dad got me a hooker last night because he had a business dinner and he didn't want to leave me alone," I said as nonchalantly as I could, hoping that my attitude would only make them envious.

Immediately, the room's atmosphere turned to static—transforming me from a pariah to the center of attention. Their grievances were instantly set aside. Each of them had a different question. "Was she brunette?" François asked. How old was she? Was she wearing perfume? What was her body like?

Then Axel, who was pudgy and awkward, asked, "Well, what about the cast? What did she do with the cast?"

"She signed it," I answered facetiously. In my complete infatuation, I had forgotten to ask her. As I scanned their faces, each one fixated on me and what I had to tell them about Natalie, I was filled with gratitude toward her for helping me regain my place among my friends.

All at once, my past infractions were deleted from the record. It was no longer of any importance whether I doubted the spiritual power of LSD or walked too heavily on my heels. I had found a position that protected me and made it easy for them to overlook my flaws. They were immediately spellbound by the prostitute I had conjured for them, and as simply as that I was released from the solitary confinement they had imposed on me.

Marco, standing by himself, didn't look up as I fielded their questions. Each answer I gave was intended as a special rebuke to his aggression. I wanted him to know that he hadn't affected me. I could still taste the anger that his lunges at me had provoked, and I felt victorious.

A few days later I was back at the Geneva airport waiting for my flight to New York for Easter vacation. Although the Pan Am staff gave me the same considerations for my cast that they had on my flight back to Lausanne, I no longer needed special treatment. It had become lighter, and I had grown so used to it that it had become an afterthought. It was only when I looked down and saw it that I

remembered that it was still part of my body. My upcoming appointment with Dr. Roth to have it removed was more frightening than
keeping the cast would be. I didn't want to think what my leg would
look like after three months in plaster or how I would be able to walk
again on two normal legs. Dad's driver, Attilio, met me at the airport
and helped me into the car.

My greeting in the front hall under the chandelier was as enthusiastic
as it had been at Christmas. If my mother and siblings had grown
accustomed to my absence, they didn't show it. Mom embraced me
and held on to me. She asked me so many questions at once, I could
barely answer any of them. Tim lugged my suitcases upstairs. Danny
showed me the glasses he had been prescribed, which resembled
mine. Eileen wanted me to listen to records with her in her room.
They had already finished dinner, but Mom had saved a plate for
me.

We sat in the living room and stared at the fire in the lulls between
their questions and my answers. "Aren't you warm, Jon?" my mother
asked, noticing that my pinstriped winter overcoat that went below
the knee was still buttoned. "Why don't you take your coat off?" At
school we never removed our coats when we entered or left rooms
or buildings. We barely noticed we were wearing them or were too
stoned to care about trivial things like layers. She came over to help
me out of it, but I resisted. I could tell that my resistance to feeling
the same temperature she did was irksome to her. Keeping my coat
on in our living room felt essential to me at that moment, as if it were
an indispensable part of my independence. I was almost sixteen and
had done so many things I couldn't reveal to her. Wearing my coat
indoors was a smaller symbol of my maturity.

After dessert I went upstairs and lay down on my old bed. Tim
said, "Listen to this," as he put on a Johnny Winter record. "Have
you ever heard someone play that fast?" he asked.

"Too fast for me," I said and started to undress in the closet. I
was too tired to unpack, and rummaged through the green bureau
drawers for pajamas until I found a pair I could still fit my good leg
into, ripping open the other seam to accommodate the cast. Mom

knocked and asked if she could come in. She went into the closet and started folding the clothes I had just taken off and then insisted on tucking me in as if I were ten years old. Before falling asleep I tried to tell Tim about my new friends in the Annex and why they were really in school in Switzerland, but we both fell asleep before I got to the contraband.

"Who's Natalie?" Mom asked sweetly the next day. "A girl from school?"

I realized my mistake instantly: sorting through my clothes, Mom had discovered the piece of paper with Natalie's name and phone number on it, which I'd left in the pocket of my green velvet pants.

"No, she's a girl I met at one of the weekend dances that École Nouvelle had with the girls' schools around Lausanne," I said, making it up as I went along, praying she wouldn't probe any further.

"Oh," she said. "Did you take her out after that? Tell me about her. Where is she from?"

"She's American actually. From somewhere in Florida. We went out for ice cream the day after we met." I was in dangerous territory.

"Oh, that's nice. Do you like her?" she asked.

"She's all right. I might call her again when I get back."

"Isn't Odeon a Paris exchange? Why would a girl from Florida studying in Switzerland have a telephone number with a Paris prefix?" she asked.

"I don't know," I said, unable to look at her, ashamed by my carelessness.

Then Mom changed the subject as if the whole matter was unimportant, although I knew she was not one to let that big a lead drop. The prospect of a further discussion filled me with horror. Instead we reviewed our plans for the next day to meet in the city at Dr. Roth's office to have my cast removed. She said she had errands to run in the morning but she would meet me and be there for the unveiling of my new leg. I walked around for the rest of the day in a trance of the doomed.

That night in bed Tim and I listened to Mom and Dad's voices rising in their bedroom and travel down the hall toward ours. At first it sounded like a normal conversation, but then it escalated into a series of screams. When Mom's high-pitched shrieks made her sound as if she were being tortured, I got out of bed and inched down the hall. I couldn't make out all of what they were saying, but I could hear Paris repeated over and over again and that was enough. I knew with a dull sense of guilt what their fight was about.

In a state of dread, I sat on the carpet outside of their room and tried imagining where they were standing. Was she facing the wall with her hands covering her face, unable to look at him? Was he next to her attempting to console her, or was he standing his ground in the middle of the room denying everything? Not being able to picture them made the anguish more intense. If he spoke, I couldn't hear him. For a second I debated knocking on the door, but my instinct told me that that would only make it worse. My legs started to shake in the near dark. My hands were skittery. I was in a state of panic.

I began to imagine what Dad's revenge on me might be and stopped trembling, becoming rigid with fear. For someone who had reminded me hundreds of times about the importance of paying attention to details, casually leaving a piece of paper with the name and number of a prostitute who my father had procured and paid for qualified as a mortal failing. I pictured his flabbergasted, red face and could already hear his denunciation. Although he had never actually shouted at me, preferring mockery as his sharpest weapon, I feared that this time might be different.

The next morning I drove into the city with Dad for the cast removal. He didn't say a word, didn't even look at me. He shuffled his papers impatiently without reading them, fiddled with the reading glasses that slid down his nose, and kept reminding Attilio to "caress the brakes." When we were almost in the garage at the Pan Am Building, he asked if I would have dinner with him that night at Chez Laurent, his favorite restaurant. The invitation filled me with nausea. The idea of being publicly chastised by Dad, in addition to losing the protection of the plaster, left me feeling doubly vulnerable.

As if I were about to part company with an ally, I made my last trip in my cast to Sam Goody's record store. At the store I flipped through the rock-and-roll bins restlessly. I went to other sections too but neither the blues nor jazz calmed me down either. I left without buying anything and walked dejectedly to Dr. Roth's office.

Mom came in and sat next to me in the waiting room. I tried to control my nervousness and not let it show. She was composed and didn't reveal any of the previous night's anguish. "Are you afraid?" she asked.

"Very. It protected me. I've gotten attached to it. I want to keep the pieces," I said.

"You do?" she asked. I looked fondly at the green sock she had knitted in the car ride after the accident. I had worn it more than any other piece of clothing. I wanted to save it even if it did have bits of dirt and grit packed into it.

Dr. Roth came out, shook our hands, and ushered me into his office. "Let's take a quick X-ray just to make sure the bones set as they were supposed to," he said. I lay down on the cold metal table. The nurse placed the metal apron over my chest, and the machine whirred and clanked above my leg.

I closed my eyes and imagined that the machine could not only see through my skin but could see into my core. It could detect that leaving Natalie's number in my pocket, not throwing it away, was an act of aggression, not a mistake. The machine could punish me with its rays, display my transgressions for the world, especially my father, to see. My innocence was a ruse, it said. I knew what my sloppiness could do, it said. I had broken the unspoken code of secrecy between men, whether I did or didn't know of its existence. I should have known. I was guilty of all charges.

A few minutes later Dr. Roth came back in with the film and pointed to where the break had been. "Typically, in an accident like this, the bones grow back stronger than they were in the first place. That means," he said, pausing for effect, "that if you're going to break it again, you'll have to do it in a different spot." He laughed at his own joke, although I was sure he had made it many times before but couldn't help marveling at how the broken body healed. Nothing felt funny to me, especially not his stupid remark.

As I lay on the table, he walked over to the metal cabinet where he kept his tools and returned with a circular saw. He moved the blade along the outside of my leg and then down the inner leg to my ankle bone. I felt nothing sharp, just the heat of it on my skin. Then he came back with a spreader, a crude instrument that looked like a jumbo can opener. When he had pried it open enough, he pushed his fingers in and raised my withered leg gingerly out of its white casing. Very slowly and deliberately he bent my knee and rotated my foot in a circle. Even those small movements felt unnatural. The leg had lost all its maneuverability.

The nurse handed the broken bits of the cast to us in a paper bag as we left. As Mom shepherded me back to Dad's office she asked, "You don't really want to keep this, do you?"

"No, I suppose not," I said.

"So let's pitch it. We can't save everything," she said, and dropped it into the first garbage can we passed. Mom was a hoarder by nature, so I interpreted this as a vestige of the previous night's anger. I felt a quick pang of nostalgia for it and then put it out of my mind as we rode the elevator to the forty-fifth floor.

Mom abandoned me in the vestibule of Dad's office with my cane and two normal shoes. She kissed me quickly and didn't linger. Carefully, I walked down the vacant hall to my uncle's office and stood looking at the dusk settle over the city. The sky was streaked by the last colorful mists of light. Waiting for Dad to finish his phone call, I slipped my new foot out of its shoe and nervously moved it around in a circle as Dr. Roth had done. I felt as vulnerable as my newly mended limb. When Dad finished his phone call, the door opened. He stood in the doorway and glanced at my leg and then me. "Let's go eat," he said plainly.

I waited while he collected his folders and reports and stuffed them into his canvas briefcase. I trailed him down the hallway, my leg aching, feeling punished even before he started in on me.

Chez Laurent was a bastion of classic French cuisine. Robert, the maître d', looked up from his reservation book over his perfectly positioned half-glasses as we entered. "Who is this boy, Arnold?" he asked, referring to me.

"Jonathan," Dad said.

"'Ah, yes the French talker. Your father has told me about you," he said.

"*Oui,*" I answered. Dad gave me an imploring look that I knew meant I was to speak more French.

"Tell me," he said in French. "Tell me where you're studying again. Your Dad told me, but I don't remember."

"I am at the École Nouvelle. Lausanne," I answered, showing off as much of the language as I could to appease Dad, being especially talkative given the perilous situation. I calculated that expansiveness might reduce the number of blows I would receive.

"Ah, Lausanne," Robert said in French. "They have funny accents there, don't they? They speak like their cows if their cows could speak," he said derisively.

"Yes, so true," I answered in French. "My friends and I can't help mimicking the accent. If we do it for long enough, we actually start to like it!"

"*Ils parlent comme ça,*" he said, imitating the melodious lilt of their speech. I was impatient to end the conversation as he laughed with the condescension of a displaced Parisian. Showing us to Dad's usual red-leather booth, he added with a flourish, "It was worth the investment, Arnold. Your son speaks French very well."

As soon as we sat down and were handed the oversized menus, Dad turned to me and snarled under his breath so no one could hear him, "You little putz," reminding me how many words for "idiot" there were in Yiddish. "How could you do that to me?" He gave me a look as if he were suffering physically. "The one thing I said to you was that you must not let your mother find out. That would include leaving a piece of paper in your pants pockets with a girl's name and a *Parisian* phone number on it. How could you be so stupid?" He seethed at me between his clenched teeth, searching my face as if

I might have a legitimate answer. I had never seen him so furious. I thought he might slap me.

"I just forgot it was there. I'm sorry. I'm sorry. I didn't want her to find it. I really didn't," I rushed to explain, to apologize, and I believed it as much as I had ever believed anything I'd ever said although I knew she had gone through and emptied my pockets before. Whether he introduced me to Ingrid and Natalie for my own good or to win me back as his son or something even more peculiar, I had never meant to expose him.

"And if the piece of paper wasn't enough, even if I could explain my way out of that, you told Eric too," he said.

"What do you mean?" I asked him in shock.

"Well, let me explain because obviously you are too dense to get it. You tell Eric. Eric for whatever idiotic reason tells Ellen, and Ellen calls your mother and tells her. Did you not guess that would happen?" he asked, drilling me with his bulging brown eyes. "Well, didn't you? Didn't it ever occur to you when and to whom Eric would repeat it?"

"I'm sorry. I'm sorry."

"Of course you're sorry now. Why weren't you sorry then?" he asked, letting the question hang in the air. "Take me through your thinking here, Jon. Were you hoping to impress him? I could understand that. But the paper is blunt stupidity!" I was ashamed and sorry. I hung my head and fidgeted with my liberated foot under the table.

"Does your puny adolescent brain have any idea how much your mother despises me right now? Or is that what you had in mind? If you want us to split up, you're doing a fine job. Well done," he added sarcastically. "She's yours. You wanted to keep her for yourself all along, didn't you? Well, you can have her," he stated venomously, his past jealousies of her intimacy with me showing through.

"No, I don't want that. I want you to stay married," I said.

"You have a strange way of showing it," he said.

I noticed then that my father looked exhausted. Obviously, he had barely slept the night before. His lower lip curled over and quivered, and his eyes were marbled. Did he really mean what he was saying? Would they separate because of me? The idea filled me with despair and guilt. I repeated to myself, "This was not your idea, this was not your idea." I didn't forget Natalie's number in my pocket on purpose. It was an accident. Natalie's face became distorted as I tried to remember her unmarred by the consequences of my negligence.

"I'm sorry, Dad," I said. I didn't know what else to say. "I blurted it out to Eric the first time I stayed at the Mitnicks' because I thought he hated me. He repeated it to his friends, and I knew I was in deep trouble—but I never imagined he would tell his mother. They barely speak, from what I saw."

"Is that why you never went back to their house?" he asked.

"Yes," I said.

"Just as well," he said. "Ellen complained about how you never finished the food on your plate. "

"I'm sorry," I said again.

"I forgive you even if she'll never forgive me," he granted, but his forgiveness felt superficial.

"She said she wants a divorce, but I don't believe she means it. She has said that before. We obviously have different ideas about what love is," he added. "Hers are romantic and pure. Ethereal. Mine are more practical, let's say. I never pretended that I was perfect." He was downplaying everything. *Practical* did not justify his frequent flirtations and the exploits he claimed, true or not.

"That's why I told you when I sent you the first time, whatever she called herself, that your mother must never find out. Didn't you believe me?" He was pleading. Since I didn't know the answer, I wasn't sure what to say. Unconsciously, I reached again for my foot under the table and played with it. I manipulated it from side to side as if it were a gear that with the right movement would make me invisible and permit me to slither away.

The dinner we had ordered sat on our plates and stared back at us. He had a few bites of a perfectly grilled steak. I probed mine with my fork and pushed it around the plate. It tasted like sawdust even with the béarnaise sauce that I loved. I forced myself to swallow as much as I could. The rest of the meal was silent aside from the metal noise of silverware. I heard other diners in other booths laughing and clinking wineglasses as from a great distance, enclosed in our own capsule of misery. For once Dad didn't comment on or notice how little I ate.

They weren't really going to divorce, I told myself. He just said it to scare me. I glanced at him out of the corner of my eye. He was sullen and defeated, staring into his lap. I'd never seen him so raw.

"The least you could do is eat your food, Jon. You haven't gained an ounce. What's wrong with you? You're as flimsy as you were three or four years ago," he added, and then squeezed my left upper arm. "Chicken wing," he pronounced it.


Later, in the dark, I saw Eric's treacherous face. How could Dad have expected me to keep a secret like that? Then the bedroom door opened and I could smell my mother's perfume. She pulled the sheets up over Tim's shoulders in the lower bunk. She climbed up on the arm of the chair and stretched the blanket over me and stroked my hair. I knew she was the one who I had truly betrayed. A mass of guilt calcified in my chest. I wanted to hurl it out and beg her to forgive me, but I couldn't utter a word and each time she touched my hair it hurt.

The next morning Mom took me out to buy new pants to replace the pairs that she had split at the seams to make room for the cast. She said they were unsalvageable. Driving to the department stores in White Plains had been one of our favorite activities together, but that day our journey was somber. She played the Dylan Thomas cassette, and he droned through the car stereo. I hadn't heard the tape in a while, and his voice sounded heavier than before. Maybe the world was more serious and painful than I thought. His voice sank into me as he read the poem about his father who sat alone on a bluff, soaking up the last light, growing more vulnerable and distant, dying slowly and quietly above the sea.

As Mom drove, I waited miserably in the passenger seat for a lecture about Natalie. I could already hear her sanctimonious voice extolling the sanctity of love, the beauty of the naked human body, and desire in its pure, native state as the balance to my vulgar actions and my father's corrupting influence. All of the beliefs that Dad had colluded with me to betray. Instead, we sat in a guilt-ridden, nervous silence I could tolerate for only so long.

"Are you and Dad going to divorce?" I finally asked.

"Why do you ask that? Is that what he told you?"

"Yes," was all I could say.

"No, no, dear. It's not like that. I was furious with him and hurt, but that's all. Couples disagree all the time. Don't give it another thought." She turned to me, giving me her most glittering smile, the one that could sell anything to anyone, the one that blotted out all other prospects as I returned to school.

# chapter 13

A month later I flew from Geneva to Madrid to meet my parents for my sixteenth birthday. In spite of the trouble my visit home had caused, I was excited to see them again, hoping that they had fully recovered from that anguished night. In spite of my desire to escape them, I still wanted to be with them, even if only to be their intermediary, their buffer, their diplomat. That was the role in which I felt most useful and valued.

They had secured permission for me to miss my classes on Thursday and Friday and join them for a long weekend. Their arrival was booked for Thursday morning, so they would be at the hotel by the time my plane landed. On two solid feet, my leg much stronger than before, I walked confidently out of the terminal and gave the taxi driver the address. I could barely recognize the word *gracias* the way he pronounced it because of the Castilian accent's heavy lisp. Arriving at the front desk to find out which room my parents were in, I felt proud of my ability to navigate the world.

The reservation clerk repeated our last name out loud and took a ledger from the shelf behind him. He ran his index finger down the list of arrivals for the day and looked back at me, shaking his head. "I don't see a reservation for your parents or you today," he said in a pan European English accent.

"Please check again," I requested, feeling prickly hot in my shirt and jacket.

"Yes, I see your reservation is for tomorrow, not today," he said.

"Are you sure?" I asked. The room had started shaking, and I felt shock waves of fear in my neck and shoulders.

"Yes, certainly. But don't worry, we still have rooms available. You can stay here tonight and your parents will arrive tomorrow."

Walking toward the room, I was perplexed—somehow I must have confused the dates. What was I going to do alone in a giant city where I didn't speak the language and didn't know anyone? I sat on the bed and unfolded the map. I found the street the hotel was on and saw that it was close to the Prado Museum. I vaguely remembered Nathan telling me about it when he showed me his book of Goya etchings. "Jonny, if you ever get the chance, go see the Goyas at the Prado Museum," he'd said. I buried the command until that moment, so I had at least one destination for the day.

There was no reason to call my parents. They'd arrive the next day and it would only upset them to know that I was there alone. I could go to the Prado and walk along the broad avenues I had seen from the taxi. The April air was fresh. Purple blossoms weighed down the branches on the jacaranda trees. My leg was regaining its former resilience, and I felt carefree enough to stroll along the boulevards designed for the triumphant processions of armies led by the fascist Generalissimo Francisco Franco, who had ruled Spain since 1939 and was still dictator.

After an hour's walk I reached the museum and headed straight to the Goya rooms. The first painting I saw showed a crowd of peasants tearing open their ruffled white shirts as a squad of soldiers was about to fire on them. The horrible scene reminded me that I wasn't a valiant traveler but a boy about to turn sixteen who was trying and failing to be brave. Goya's scene of the brutal massacre made me queasy.

From that moment on I felt steadily worse. My leg began to ache from the long walk. I was hungry. The paintings started to blur together, and I began to feel nauseous and dizzy. I knew I had to leave the museum as quickly as I could. I took the first available exit, which opened into the broiling sun, and staggered to a bench under one of the branches to catch my breath and calm myself down. The little street I was on smelled of bus and taxi fumes, and I couldn't locate it on the map. Beginning to panic, I managed to find a bodega for some water and an empanada, but that turned my stomach.

The parade of taxis passing by gave me an idea. Hadn't Dad told me that taxi drivers knew where to find girls? Suddenly, I wanted Natalie again, her comfort and affirmation. The idea quickly grew into a compulsion that gripped me completely, an antidote to the loneliness that was spreading through me.

I told myself that this time I had to be more careful with the details so that my mother would not find out. Dad wouldn't care or would herald my independence, or maybe he would have said that the taxi driver story was just a myth he had made up to amuse me. If you'd wanted a girl, you should have gone back to the hotel, I could hear him say. Even in his absence, he was able to second-guess me. I heard his voice suggesting alternatives that I hadn't considered, but I ignored them.

I formulated a plan. The urgency became a necessity, an obsession that was a sloppy mixture of desire, disorientation, and a curiosity I couldn't master. I looked at the blossoms, the sky, the sun. Everything other than the attention that Natalie's counterpart would pay me felt trivial.

I stood up in the street and stuck my hand in the air. A taxi pulled over and I got in. From the way I said *Hola* he could tell I was American. "I spend two years in the Bronx," he said. "A horrible place. Not like this," he said, gesturing at the wide streets through the windshield and the colorful blossoms. "Where are you going?" he asked. His English surprised me. I wasn't expecting to have to explain myself in my own language. That made my question seem sordid. Still, I asked: "Do you know where I can meet a girl?"

"How old?" was his only response. I wasn't sure whether he was checking my age or the age of the girl I wanted.

"My age?" I asked him.

"How old are you? Fourteen? That's hard to find," he said, chuckling. "Don't worry. I know where to go," he said. I sat back in the seat, uncertain whether I was making the worst decision in my life or merely continuing the mistakes that had already been made for me.

We drove through the streets in what felt like an expanding spiral. Whichever street we turned down, the jacaranda hung over us. The buildings became progressively more pockmarked as more and more laundry hung from the spindly racks of cramped balconies. The taxi pulled up to a nondescript apartment building. The driver walked with me to a panel of doorbells. He pushed one and announced his name in a rasping voice. The door buzzed open.

The lobby was dark, but as soon as I entered the lights flashed on automatically. The elevator in the corner with its wire mesh window sucked me toward it. When I exited on the seventh floor I saw a thin slice of light at the end of a dark corridor. A modestly dressed middle-aged woman with a gleaming gold cross caught crookedly inside her cleavage greeted me and gestured for me to sit down on the uneven sofa covered in plastic. The apartment was mostly unfurnished. She wrote down how many pesetas it was because she could tell I couldn't speak Spanish. I dug the bills out of my pocket and put them on the table. She asked me if I wanted a soda and left the room.

A few minutes later a girl walked in from one of the side doors wearing a baby-blue satin slip and a matching ornate bra. She had long brown ringlets and pimply skin. She placed her hand on my leg and said something to me in Spanish I couldn't understand. *"Vous parlez français?"* I asked her. She shook her head and left the room.

I sat alone for a few minutes, and then another girl entered from another door. She looked like the sister of the first girl. She put her arm on my shoulder and plucked at the hair on my neck. Again, I asked if she spoke French. She said no and walked out. I didn't know if there were more girls about to enter from other doors or if any of them spoke a language I could understand. I felt a great need to communicate and be understood, to confide in someone, to confess why I was there and hear what she might say to soothe me. Natalie's few sentences ricocheted around my head.

Then a third girl entered. She looked different from the other two. Her dark hair was dyed a shade of blond that looked auburn in the late-afternoon light. I asked if she spoke French. *"Un peu,"* she said. She was the one. Even the simplest dialogue might relieve me of my malaise. I thought of resting my head against her throat and feeling the safety I had felt with Natalie. When she stood up, I wondered if she was older than I was or even younger.

The madam came back in and asked me which girl I wanted. I held up three fingers, and she nodded. She motioned to me to follow her and led me to another room that was empty except for a doctor's examining table covered with a sheet of white paper. She positioned me against it and left the room. A moment later the girl who spoke a few words of French came in. She stood next to me, leaning back against the table, and stared at her bare feet. "Where did you learn French?" I asked in French, hoping to start a conversation.

"*École,*" she said. She seemed as scared to look at me as I was to look at her.

As she stood paralyzed beside me, I realized that I was afraid of touching her. Worse, whatever conversation I hoped to have with her would never happen. I felt cheated, almost indignant. Didn't she know that she was supposed to take charge of me? Had she never done this before? Was I supposed to teach her, touch her first? The thought disturbed me. I tried to catch her eyes, but she wouldn't look up from the floor. I brushed my fingers across her shoulder shyly. Since there was no reaction, I kissed her cheek, remembering how Ingrid had kissed me so lightly.

Without acknowledging me, she took the straps off her shoulder and her slip slid to the floor. She lifted herself onto the table and lay down on her back and spread her legs. She still ignored me. I climbed on top of her, and we were like two children, one lying on top of the other, each of us wanting to hide. When she felt my erection, she put me inside her and put her weightless hands on my back. From the way her head flopped to the side I could tell she was gazing toward the window hoping that the blossoms on the branches would somehow carry her away. I came immediately and was instantly and profoundly ashamed of myself. I lurched down from the table as soon as I could move my legs. She said nothing and continued to avoid looking at me.

I put my clothes on quickly, wanting to forget every detail of the room: the table, the coarse sheet of paper, the mute girl with her fear of me and her naked feet. My clothes felt rank and scratchy. On the street I stuck my fingers down my throat to force my loathsomeness out of me. I was ashamed by my desire for her, my loneliness, the city, and Dad's offhand story about taxi drivers that I turned into a prescription. I felt desecrated. My body was rotten. Even the people who were supposed to love and protect me were putrid. I wanted to rip my skin off. What had I done? How had I done it? Who had led me there? How had I led myself there? The poor girl was only the latest, most obvious part of the answer. The thinness in myself, the thinness that I was accused of, gave me a giant's appetite for solace. A hunger that was beyond my ability to control. The nourishment my stomach didn't crave, my brain ached for.

As if my body were rebelling against my mind, I was trembling when I got out of the taxi and stepped back inside the hotel. Trying to calm myself, I drank cups of water from the tap and took deep breaths sitting on the bed with my hands on my knees, but the shaking didn't stop. It felt as if my brain and body were separating and these spastic movements were a sign that my legs were trying to run away from me. Spasm after spasm ripped through my body.

In my head I heard myself repeat my consolations: You're all right, Jon. You're all right. If I said it enough times, maybe I could believe it. Maybe my heart would slow down. I was sweating and disoriented and wriggled to the floor so I wouldn't fall. There was a darkness in my head that I couldn't see through. I had become a dissipated version of my father. Was I as degraded and desperate as he was? I knew then that I had to change. If I didn't, there'd be more McEnerys, more Ingrids. A parade of them to trample me. I'd never escape the monsters who would feed on me.

My shaking slowed down enough that I could take my clothes off and have a shower. I wanted to be rid of the brothel smell and the madam's foul perfume. With the towel wrapped around me, I sat on the floor in a stupor. I thought about flying back to Switzerland, leaving for the airport before my parents landed so they wouldn't see me in this condition, but I didn't even have the energy to climb into bed. I fell asleep on the floor.


Mom and Dad arrived the next morning. I remembered little about their visit except how hollow and listless I felt driving through the endless, nameless streets with the pretty purple blossoms overhead pretending that I was enjoying the splendor of the city as much as they did so they could not guess at my revulsion.

*Part 3*

# chapter 14

I spent one more year at École Nouvelle, and when I returned to finish high school at an American boarding school, I could barely speak to a girl. I felt that everyone could see through my outer layers to a corrupt center that was glaringly visible. The revulsion I felt in Madrid after I met the unnamed girl in her unnamed suburb never entirely left, haunting me long after I returned from Europe.

During my year of boarding school, I lived in a small house on the edge of the campus with four other boys. Compared with the motley student body at École Nouvelle they were a normal group of kids from familiar places: Long Island, somewhere in the South, and nearby Massachusetts. To fit in with them I tried to become normal too: no French, no bizarre adventures. I had grown a little and was well over eighty pounds, so my appearance was a little more normal too.

When I graduated from boarding school, I convinced my parents to let me take a year off to write a novel in Paris before starting at St. John's College in Annapolis, Maryland. Being a fiction writer was a dream I'd nurtured for years but never tested, and what better laboratory than Paris. In addition, I argued that I wasn't ready for another educational transition. Including one year at a local day school, I had attended three schools in four years. They agreed on the condition that I have a structure for my time. We decided that I would enroll in French classes at the Alliance Française to consolidate my fluency.

I found a studio apartment on the Left Bank behind the Panthéon and had most of my meals at the Café Panthéon on the rue Soufflot. For fifty francs a day I could afford enough food to sustain me and have change left over to play pinball. I spent many afternoons at the machines because it was almost immediately clear that I couldn't write a novel. Instead I read Proust. I walked around the city end-lessly and, rather than rock and roll, listened to classical music on my cassette player at night to insulate me from the failure of my literary effort and put myself to sleep. My favorite was *The Four Seasons* by Vivaldi. Usually, by the end of "Spring," the first movement, with its fluted birds, warm updrafts of air, and the harvest celebration, I was out. The year passed in a benign blur, and the only conclusion I was able to draw from it was that I was without any talent as a novelist.

Upon my return, I was ready to spend the summer at home before starting college in Annapolis. There had been some additions to the house in my absence. There was a new abstract painting in the living room and a silver Möbius strip that rocked back and forth on the piano. Faint percussive music reverberated in an upstairs bedroom. David Bowie. Since Tim wasn't back from boarding school and rarely returned, it had to be coming from Eileen's room, as Danny didn't listen to that kind of music. It had been Eileen who'd filled me in on the deeper changes in the house, having to do with our parents: "They are playing cat-and-mouse games with each other all the time. She is whispering into the phone in the back stairs. I have no idea who she's talking to. He's not here much. On the weekends the house is full of strangers."

Soon I saw this for myself. People much younger than our parents wandered around the property as if it were a public park. These were not our parents' close friends who we had grown up with. They were strangers who wore tight-ribbed turtlenecks and bell-bottoms and spoke in rapturous language about gurus and spiritual fulfillment.

One day in May soon after my nineteenth birthday while I was upstairs in Eileen's bedroom listening to music, a metal clinking from the hall below announced that Mom was home, because she always dropped her car keys in the brass ashtray on the front hall table. I greeted her in the hallway. I had hoped to regain some trust between us, but in the days since I'd been back, I'd remained wary, expecting the types of invasive questions that had always made me squirm. Any girlfriends yet? Anyone special? Even unasked, the questions gnawed at me. I revealed as little as possible, and even so I worried that I had said too much. Just in case, I said almost nothing. Was it fair for a mother to want to know all of her nineteen-year-old son's personal information? I didn't want to be hard-hearted, but what else could I be? I was unable to imagine a compromise in which I could be sincere about some things and discreet about others.

"A letter came for you from the government. I think you should open it," she said, and pushed it into my hands. "It looks official and important."

The words "Selective Service System" were printed in the upper left corner of the envelope. As my mother watched, I read the letter that said I had been given a draft number, 295, which was very low on the table. Nonetheless, it requested that I contact my local draft board immediately. That was impossible, I thought to myself. The Vietnam War was over, wasn't it? I remembered reading about a peace treaty in the *International Herald Tribune*. And of all people, how could they want an underweight boy with glasses? Like every American my age, I had heard wild tales of draft dodging, from pretending to be queer to drinking enough coffee to elevate your heart rate beyond levels stable enough to patrol the Vietnamese jungles.

"I'm being drafted, Mom," I said to her. She looked up at me. I was at least five inches taller than she was.

"You won't have to go, but what a shameful war!" she said with outrage. I showed her the letter. I knew she hated the Vietnam War as if it were a person who had betrayed her idea of herself.

When Dad came home he agreed there must be an error. "The draft's over. This must be some crazy army mistake. Remember the snafus I used to tell you boys about? Sending guys to serve in the Arctic Circle with safari kits and shipping insulated suits to the Pacific? And if it isn't a mistake, I know people on the town draft board. I think I can get you out of it," he said. Later that night at dinner, having given it some more thought, he added, "Just in case, why don't you make an appointment with Dr. Diamond and see what he has to say. I'm sure he's dealt with this kind of nonsense before. Maybe there's a medical excuse he can provide you with."

I made an appointment and drove to my old pediatrician's office a few days later. It smelled and looked as it always had. The odor of rubbing alcohol saturated the air. The little chairs and tables in the waiting room for the younger patients were in their usual places; the issues of *Highlights* were left open to the pages filled with jokes and riddles. Unusual for me, I felt like a giant sitting among the Lilliputians.

Dr. Diamond opened the door and walked toward me with his hand extended as if I were an adult. "Good to see you, Jonathan," he said.

"So how are you doing? How's your eating? Take those clothes and shoes off so I can get a thorough look at you," he said.

"I'm not really here for a regular checkup," I said as I undressed.

"Well, we'll talk about that in a minute. Stand here so I can measure you. Five feet seven and a half. That makes you taller than your father, doesn't it?" he asked.

"I think so. By a hair," I said. "I got a draft notice. That's why I'm here."

"Oh, I see. Step on the scale. Let's see how your weight is?"

"Ninety-four pounds. Not bad," he said.

The number on the scale astonished me. I could have sworn that the last time I had weighed myself the needle had pushed past my unattainable number, the one-hundred-pound threshold that he had once inspired me to attain. How could I have made such a mistake, or had it been wishful thinking? "Are you sure that's right?" I asked him. "I thought I was over a hundred pounds."

"Close but not quite. Which is good news: you don't weigh enough to be in the army. A hundred pounds is their minimum. Maybe there's something else you could do if you wanted to serve. I will be happy to certify that to your draft board," he said.

I didn't hear another word he said. I was dumbstruck by the knowledge that this time my body had rescued me—proud of it in spite of its hardness, in spite of the prominence of my hip bones and my skinny wrists. In light of this, it took on more useful properties such as versatility and uniqueness. Yes, I was slight, but slightness had advantages. I felt giddy.

As Dr. Diamond rambled on, asking me about college, I began to see myself escaping from the fortress of my childhood. I didn't need its protection any longer. I had my own solidity. I was taller than my mother and even taller than my father. I spoke another language and had lived alone on another continent. The features of my body wouldn't prevent me from growing up. Despite my father's concerns about my weight and my future, I was beginning to display adult attributes even if I wasn't a full-grown man.

At dinner that night I announced the good news of my visit to Dr. Diamond as if it were a vindication of my eating habits. Mom's eyes were misty, and Dad fidgeted in his chair in front of the giant yellow-orange impressionist painting of the Duomo that towered over him. He appeared small beneath it, a lowly parishioner slumped in his chair, hamming up a forced state of relaxation.

"That's great, Jon. I have an announcement too but maybe not as good as yours. I found you a job for the summer. Starting tomorrow. I want you to work for Wells Television and learn about our business at the lowest level. I've already discussed it with Harry. You'll go see him in the morning and he'll get you suited up. You're going to be a television attendant at NYU Hospital. You'll be paid for it of course, and you'll be part of the Wells force," he said. I'd never heard him refer to his employees before as a kind of ant army lugging television sets across America. It was far better than serving in the real army, so I agreed without protest.

As much as I admired my Dad's business acumen, I didn't really understand what he did day to day. From the bits and pieces he reported to us at the dinner table from when we were very young—of sales meetings, group escapades and conventions in other cities—it was impossible for me to visualize what his daily activities consisted of. They seemed to parade by us in a fog of postures, boasts, disappointments, and deals salvaged at the last minute. As if those tall tales were connected to actual wisdom, he repeated certain axioms frequently: "A great salesman only starts selling when the customer says no."

The next morning his car dropped me outside a nondescript garage on a side street off Park Avenue South. Inside there were vans suspended in the air on hoists, tools scattered on workbenches, and oil-soaked rags that stank. On the wall were pinup-girl calendars left over from previous years that hadn't been recycled. No one was working, and I wondered if I was in the right place until I heard a gruff voice yelling at someone in the background. "What the fuck do you think you're doing? Who told you? Who gave you permission?"

A telephone receiver was slammed down, and then there was the *plink* as it flipped off the cradle and clattered on the metal surface of Harry's standard-issue desk. I walked toward the swearing voice a little stunned. I'd never heard that word used by an adult before. Harry appeared in the doorway of the lone office. He smiled at me as if he might not be the man who had cursed. The top of his head was hidden by cylinders of cigar smoke. He said in a calm, raspy voice, "I hope you didn't hear that. Those yokels don't know what's going on around here. So, Arnold told me that you wanted to work this summer and has entrusted you to me," he said, pronouncing my father's name as though there were an *h* after the *a* and making it sound German. "Do you know what we do?"

"You put televisions in sick people's rooms and collect the money," I said hopefully.

"Right. Two dollars a day for black-and-white and three for color. Plus seven percent tax. How hard could it be?" he asked rhetorically, and examined my face to see if I had a question. No questions formed in my mind. "I picked a nice starter hospital for you so that you could still go in and out of the city with your Pop. No Bronx for you. NYU. Check in with Sadie at the front desk, and she'll tell you where Akash is. And please do a good job so your old man doesn't get pissed at me." He tapped me softly on the shoulder with a pretend fist.

The hospital was a giant building that extended several blocks along First Avenue. Nurses, orderlies, and doctors passed briskly in and out of the revolving doors. Each was wearing a uniform in a different style and color with stethoscopes and tongue suppressors poking out of their front pockets. Inside I saw an elderly lady wearing a blue jacket like mine. "The boss's son. My, my. Aren't you sweet," she said. "Akash is on the sixth floor. He knows you're coming, so meet him up there. Oh, and take these with you," she said, handing me a small sheaf of papers.

I rode the elevator up and got out not sure what I was looking for. At the end of a long corridor I saw a man pulling wires out of a metal cart. Akash's silver glasses frames clashed with his deep-brown skin. When he stood up, he saw me and waved me over.

"Jonathan, hello," he said, and extended his hand in a formal manner. "Welcome to the orthopedic floor. Everyone here is in a sling," he said. "But this is one of my favorites. At least they can talk." I handed him the slips Sadie had handed to me. Akash was a neat man, a little intense around the eyes. High-strung, I thought. He told me he was from Hyderabad.

"Thank you. We'll get to these later. First, let's start here." He lifted one of the sets. Attached to the bottom of it was a pole that was almost three feet long. He carried it into the adjacent room where a man lay in bed with his heavily bandaged right arm extended high over his head behind him. He was barely conscious.

"Here's the set you ordered, sir," Akash said, then slotted it into a hole at the end of a long extendable arm that put the set within a few feet of the patient's face. The arm was labeled a Wellbow, a device trademarked by my father's company. The remote control with a volume dial and a little button to push to change one of the seven channels was already clipped onto his pillow.

"Would you like that for a day or a week, sir?" Akash asked. The patient grunted and pointed with his chin to the drawer of the rolling table next to the bed. Akash extracted a twenty-dollar bill and held it up.

"A week then, sir? I'm sorry to hear that," he said. Akash tossed the change and the receipt into the drawer. With his one good hand, the patient clipped the remote control to the pillowcase next to his ear and then brought the television closer to his face. He touched it, almost caressed it, as though the set and the man were about to share the single hospital bed together and the set would whisper and coo into his ear.

"Thank you, sir," Akash said, and I trailed him out the door. I couldn't wait to leave.

"Those are the easy ones," he said. "You'll get the hang of it. It's not so bad, but it's not a life's work. I'm doing this crummy job until I finish my engineering degree this winter. Almost three years I've been doing this, but it was the only work I could find. The system is fucked. You should tell your old man that."

I nodded, and as we went from room to room throughout the day he kept delivering monologues. He had a solution for everything. If only he were running the company, the billing would be automatically added to the patient's room, the nurses would adjust the picture, the orderlies could lock in the vertical and horizontal hold, and he wouldn't have to fill out paperwork in triplicate. As he went through his litany of criticisms, I noticed how neat and self-disciplined he was. His pens were lined up in his pocket protector, his shirt was always tucked in. Akash was a serious, practical man.

Just before four, having worked our way floor by floor through the hospital, Akash said it was time to stop for tea. He led me through long hallways, past nurses' stations, and around corners to a little canteen. I sat down while he ordered his tea with a drop of milk. When he returned, a little glassy-eyed and distracted, he said, "I need to prepare you before we go to the ICU."

"What does that stand for?"

"Intensive care unit. The patients aren't just sick. Many of them are in a coma. Some have almost passed on. Their families are usually with them, and everyone is extra quiet. There are no kids, no balloons. Sometimes flowers. You can't be loud. You have to be silent. Like a butler. They need the television to get them through it. They need it so badly, but you still have to ask for the money even if you say it very, very softly."

I'd only been in a hospital once before, when Dad had caught his hand in a snowblower after he and Mom had had a big fight. Once he removed the branch that had stopped the blades, they started spinning. He had forgotten to put the gearshift in neutral, and the tips of his middle fingers hung by sinews. Reconstructive surgery had saved his index finger, but two others were left stubbed. Mom had taken me out of Adams for an hour to visit him in the hospital. I had never seen him that still before. His right hand was covered in so many bandages that it looked as if he were wearing a white catcher's mitt. He was morose, and I felt sorry for him. When Mom dropped me back at school after the visit, I could barely speak due to the melancholy that engulfed me. He was better in a few days and used his damaged hand as a gag. Whenever we had guests who asked if Danny's dog was friendly, Dad would hold up his mangled hand and, trying not to laugh, say, "Use your own judgment."

"This floor would be a good place for your first delivery," Akash said on our way to the ICU. "I don't think you could wake some of these people even if you dropped the set on them. Ready?"

I had no immediate response. What could have prepared me for something so awkward? Had my father ever done what I was about to do? Did he walk into the rooms of dying people to extract twenty dollars? Was that how he paid for my college? I couldn't think of it that way. Instead I imagined the television and the reverent yet perky tones of its newscasters and the familiar soap operas as the continuity of life. Of life itself. Television provided the accompaniment—the music, the scenery, the dialogue. Twenty bucks wasn't much for that wondrous, natural feeling.

"Yup. I'm ready."

Akash glanced at the slip that said room 919. Color. When we reached it, he knocked gently on the half-open door. I heard a gentle noise and pushed it all the way open. A white-haired lady who resembled my grandmother lay peacefully on the bed, her head turned toward the window, where a bouquet of lilies was past its peak color, like the rouge on her cheeks. Her skin was papery. She had a beatific look on her face that consoled me, as though death could be peaceful, not just violent as I had imagined. I was more comforted than shocked. A man in the visitor's chair nodded when I pointed to the Wells insignia on my jacket. We communicated in a speechless pantomime of signals and gestures. I lowered the pole into its slot, trying not to make a sound. It fit perfectly. My instinct was to flee, and I nearly left without payment, but Akash blocked my exit. The man handed me the bills and coins for a whole week in advance. Akash slipped them into a zippered pouch that he was always touching through his pocket, even when he sipped his milky tea.

I was still upset when I walked to meet Dad at his office. The contrast between the hospital and headquarters was stark. The halls were empty and hushed. The secretaries and most of the executives had left for the evening. The light was soft, not fluorescent. It was almost six o'clock, and Dad was packing up his papers. When he saw me, he beamed. We rode the elevator together and walked through the doors to the garage. He smiled, and I imagined him saying to himself, Maybe the kid isn't so useless after all. He seemed proud of me for working with him, joining his effort and learning the ropes. In the car ride home, he peppered me with questions. How many sets? How many color? How much cash? Checks? Do the math. How did we do?

"Akash says it would be easier if it was billed through the hospital. Is that true?" I asked.

"No, not at all. We'd lose control. He probably won't last long. We've learned over the years that women are the best attendants. They grouse less and don't get ruffled. They are kinder to the patients. Keep better track of the paperwork, and most of all, they don't steal. We have almost five thousand attendants, you know?" He smiled his lopsided smile.

"Did you ever have to go into a dying person's room, Dad?"

"No, I never did that. When we started this business, television barely existed. It was all radios. We had coin-operated ones that would play for an hour, and we put them in special hotels in Harlem. That was over twenty years ago. That's how it started."

"What kinds of hotels have radios that take coins?"

"Hotels by the hour. You'd bring your girl there and put a quarter in the slot. It was like your own jukebox. Jazz, blues, Sinatra, whatever your fancy. When I emptied them each night, they were full of money. I knew we had a business. But to answer your question, I stopped collecting the cash long before we went into hospitals."

For the first time I could remember, I felt respected by him. Even if it was only a passing twinge, it was warm, almost lush. Understanding what he did, working with the people who worked for him, gave me the sense of a bond between us that we had never had before. I kept the sense of it to myself to nurture it. When we got home, I ran up the stairs to the bedroom Tim and I still shared. He had just returned from boarding school. He asked me how the work was, and I grunted. I couldn't say a word.

Dad's pride in me and my encounters with very sick patients turned into weeks and then months. His satisfaction with me lasted in some form for the whole summer, but I could feel less of it each day. By Tuesday night, I wanted the week to end so badly that I would pray for it. The lists of sick people who wanted televisions were endless. The jingles of game shows and artificial sitcom laughter echoed hollowly in my ears night after night, and I started to fantasize about going back to school, studying the great texts as if they would transport me from the hospital and its sad, antiseptic hallways. Even the pleasure Dad took in the work we shared wasn't enough to pull me through the discomfort.

When my job was over, on the last car ride home, Dad told me he was grateful that I had tried so hard. Not every kid could do that, he said. He looked at me as if he meant it, and there was no joke building up that would diminish the compliment. That was one of the best feelings I'd ever had.

# chapter 15

"Arnold, you'll be pleased to hear that it's blue-crab season in Annapolis," Mom said, studying the Maryland guidebook and showing off the results of her investigation.

"You mean the blue-plate special?" he asked, barely cracking a smile.

"No, the Chesapeake Bay blue crab. And oysters too. Everything is fresh off the fishing boats this time of year," she added, paying no attention to his attempt to subvert her enthusiasm. When he started to laugh at his attempt at a joke that wasn't funny, she smirked.

We plowed through Maryland's Eastern Shore in the late afternoon of a dark, clouded day. The sky seemed lower there, resting on the tops of the hilly fields. The few birds swooped down onto the tips of the cornstalks and then took off into the distance. I loved listening to my father's banter from the backseat, especially when I wasn't the butt of it. His gentle teasing, which was different from his cynical mockery, didn't make a dent in Mom's composure.

"I think Middleton Tavern is the right spot. It's downtown next to the docks." She tilted the book sideways and traced the crooked little streets from St. John's College to the harbor. "It's walking distance from school, I think," she said. I had inherited from her the gene for no-sense-of-direction and believed that everyone, even she, had a better sense of orientation than I did. An hour later we were on the Bay Bridge crossing over onto the Maryland mainland. We could see the distant lights of the city through a blue haze.

Dad and I had researched colleges together and picked St. John's after a few Saturday mornings thumbing through a college guide. When we read through the syllabus, which consisted of original texts of philosophy and religion and mathematics without referring to secondary sources, he subtly began to push me toward it. His interest in the program took me by surprise. He was a reader of history and fiction, but I'd never seen him delving into the dialogues of Plato. Although I hadn't read any philosophy before, I was attracted to abstract ideas. They would be serious, I thought to myself, not flighty like poems and stories.

After dropping my blue suitcases in my room overlooking the state capitol, we picked our way down the little cobblestone streets to the harbor. Behind wooden fences were colonial mansions and gardens glimpsed through peepholes carved into the pickets. Some houses were from the 1700s and some were even older, but when we turned a corner into the main square, the stately past was replaced by cars, convertibles, and pickups backed up in bumper-to-bumper traffic; on the water, dinghies wedged against one another seemed to fight for access to the iron cleats on the dock.

Middleton Tavern faced the water. The porch was filled with men in suits with rep ties and weekend sailors in pink shorts, belts with whales woven into them, and boat shoes. Platters of oysters and pitchers of beer were slammed down on rickety tables by the white-shirted waiters. Throngs of people gathered around drinking cocktails on the patio. As our waiter explained: "The legislature's in town, but it's hard to tell them apart from the sailors. Except for the ties everybody here wears the same basic uniform."

The waiter, Bill, told us he came from Pittsburgh, was the oldest of eight kids, and had transferred to St. John's after his sophomore year at George Washington University. The program at St. John's required that he begin as a freshman instead of a junior, he told us.

"Why would you do something like that?" I asked him.

"Because here you study truth and justice, and if you want to participate in the world, to change the world, you have to know what those mean beginning with the Greeks," he said. I studied his face, hoping to find clues to what that really meant. I thought I knew what was true and what was just, but truth and justice by themselves felt unknowable. Bill pronounced everything he said with emphasis and certainty. He made it clear that he'd done the thinking necessary to make the assertion and there was no point in reviewing the steps. Brown curls bounced over his forehead when he spoke, his hands trembled slightly, and I could see the nicotine stains on his fingers.

"Look how that kid hustles. That's what impresses me," Dad said to me pointedly as Bill rushed away. "He probably works here three or four nights a week to pay for school. And he still has to study and have some kind of a social life. I'm not sure I could do that or you could either," he said, staring at me. "Luckily, we won't have to find out."

I felt small in my chair. It was only a week before that he had doled out praise for me, on our last ride home from work, and already he was shrinking me back to my pre-work shape. My stature fluctuated in my mind according to my father's view of me. If I had done something well, I felt larger, with my feet better planted on the floor, a plumb line extending through the center of my head down through my innards and my legs and anchoring me where I stood. It connected the loose parts of me to its central thread. If I had forgotten what I was supposed to do or didn't do it quickly enough or misplaced the details, my identity flew apart and frittered away. I couldn't hold on to the pieces or keep them together. The only conclusion I could draw from Dad's comment was that I should in some way learn from Bill how to be more like him.

"What do you do, sir, if I may ask?" Bill asked Dad, later in the meal. Without pause, Dad launched into a long discussion of the hospital television business and its market share and the number of hospitals and attendants who worked for him all over the country. His spiel didn't include any reference to sick people and how depressing it was to do the actual jobs he described. It was all numbers and sums and percentages. Despite the boisterous crowd, Bill listened as if he had no other table to wait on or oysters to deliver; he listened so raptly that not even a tidal wave would tear him away from where he stood. Occasionally, he would look in my direction to include me in the conversation, but it was clear that I was an afterthought.

Mom was used to encountering young men who wanted to flatter Dad and try to make an impression on him. She pulled the guidebook from her bag and flipped through the pages, turning a corner down here and there. At one point she leaned toward me so I could read the entry about the Naval Academy.

"You know, I was engaged to a cadet at the Naval Academy before I met your father. I've told you about him, haven't I? His name was Yale," she said.

"His name was Yale?" I asked. "What kind of name is that? No wonder you wanted me to apply there," I said, and smiled to take the edge off. She blushed. Of course, the question that lingered in the air at that moment was whether she had married the wrong man.

Meanwhile, Bill was saying, with righteous conviction: "I think there has to be a fundamental change in health care in America. That's what I want to be part of. I want to watch the universal right to medicine become the law of the land. Everybody who wants to should be able to see a doctor. In Pittsburgh, not everyone has that opportunity."

I thought about Bill long after the meal was over. He was an enigma. He'd spent two years at a different university and then threw in the towel to start over again at St. John's as a freshman, to better align himself with his ideals. I hadn't met anyone quite like him. What did it mean? If nothing else, that he was at least two years older than I was. That combined with Dad's attention to him only added to his authority. I vowed to myself that we would become friends so I might model myself on him and rise in Dad's estimation.


The St. John's campus struck me as a beautiful home. Giant oaks hundreds of years old were generously spaced among its front lawns. Some of them even had their own names and birth years pinned on them. The great lawn in the back sloped to the Severn River at least a thousand yards away. Brick paths linked the library to the classroom buildings, and dormitories faced a small quadrangle. Every window was open, and I could hear snatches of Joni Mitchell's voice and the prickly chords of an electric guitar.

Student conversation spilled from everywhere. It clustered in the small basement corners of the Federal-style school buildings and overflowed onto the quadrangle and the lawn. Everyone seemed curious, articulate, and gesticulating, appearing to make their arguments using their hands. I wondered how they found so much to say and why they needed to say it so publicly.

After my first geometry class, I started speaking with Pat. He was a big-boned kid from Oregon who wore a threadbare blue polo sweater with elbow patches that looked like they might cover real holes. There was nothing fashionable about him. He swaggered when he walked without meaning to in a way that emphasized his size. After we finished puzzling our way through the first Euclidean theorems, Pat said he needed a beer badly, and he led me between the buildings to the Little Campus Inn, a bar a few blocks away.

We spent the next seven hours ensconced in a red leather booth. The more Pat drank, the darker his eyes became and the closer together his eyebrows grew. His unshaved cheeks turned darker too, and his rugged look more foreboding. If Bill was the friend my father wanted me to have, Pat was the friend no parent would choose for their child. At first I didn't know what was dangerous about him. He told me how he had worked in a sawmill all summer to save up money for his fall expenses. He drained beer after beer. I had never seen anyone drink that much liquid without any noticeable effect or needing to pee. I could only manage one for every three of his and needed to go to the bathroom as soon as I finished it.

"They called me Youngblood," he told me without saying who "they" were. "The sawdust would live in you like a tick. You couldn't wash it out. You'd feed the planks into the saw all day and it was boring as hell, but if you took your eye off it for a second, it would cut off your hand or your arm. Happened all the time."

Whether he was exaggerating or not, renting television sets to the convalescent felt like a dalliance by comparison. I looked at his hands. His fingers were rough and his nails were bitten down as far as they could go, but that didn't stop him from chewing on them more.

"The only thing that made me not hate it and hate myself was when I got home I'd open a beer and read Fitzgerald," he said. He looked up from his glass to make sure I had understood him. "*The Great Gatsby*. I read it over and over all summer. At least five times."

He closed his eyes and began to recite, "'He smiled understandingly—much more than understandingly. It was one of those rare smiles with a quality of eternal reassurance in it, that you may come across four or five times in life.'" Pat paused for a second before continuing. "'It understood you just as far as you wanted to be understood, believed in you as you would like to believe in yourself.'" He stopped and looked up at me, and I thought for a second that he was looking for the kind of recognition the passage described, the kind of recognition that I wanted for myself. It reminded me of my father and how he spoke to me and looked at me in the back of his car after my first day of working for him.

"Not bad, Sport. Right?" he asked. His eyes opened, but they were masked and watery. The frequency with which he called me Sport increased with each beer.

"Did you know that James Joyce refers to the city of Annapolis in *Finnegans Wake*? He called it Anna's city," I said.

"He did? Good research, Sport. What other college could you use that at? Are you tight yet?" he asked. "Let's get out of here. Where's your room?"

I didn't realize until I stood up how dizzy I was. Through the cigarette smoke that sat above the smokers' heads like captions filled with fog, I could see the outline of the front door and moved toward it. Faces looked at me from other tables as I squeezed past them. Some were familiar from class. Pat put his heavy arm on my shoulder and pulled me toward the lighted clearing in front of the exit.

"Are you tight yet?" he asked me again.

The answer was obvious.


A few nights later after another session with Pat at the Little Campus that resulted in the same stupor, we decided to walk back to my room. My roommate probably wouldn't be there, I figured. He was elusive. We had met only a few times during the first week, and all I had learned about him was that he came from a small town in Virginia. When we were there at the same time, he sat quietly at his desk studying the conjugation tables of Greek verbs, but since he was there so rarely, I assumed we would have it to ourselves. Besides, we didn't have anywhere else to go.

After weaving our way back to the little brick colonial house where my room was, Pat walked me to my bed and deposited me there. I nodded off for a second, and when I opened my eyes I saw him standing in front of my closet with the door open.

"What are these?" he asked. He was holding up my green stacked-heel boots and smiling fiercely.

"You audition for *Soul Train* in these?" He smirked and let them drop to the floor. They made a clatter as they landed on the bare wood.

"What about this?" he asked. He held out the hanger with the green velvet suit on it that my father had given me money to buy in Paris a few years before. He started laughing, and it slithered to the ground as though its occupant had melted like the Wicked Witch of the West. I tried to see the suit from Pat's perspective, but it was a difficult picture of myself to imagine. It was the place where our worlds clashed, and the loud noise of that collision left me speechless and embarrassed by my advantages. This was the first time I was aware of that conflict and in spite of the alcohol the impact was abrasive.

The door opened and Bill burst in. Since our first meeting at Middleton Tavern we found we were in the same seminar and his dormitory was close to mine. He looked as surprised to be there as we were to see him. I sat up on the bed.

"I just ran into your roommate. Good luck with that motherfucker. God, he looks dim," Bill said, and stretched out on the other bed. "What the fuck is that?" he asked, pointing at the heap of fabric on the floor.

"Jonny's outfit," Pat said, referring to me. I hadn't been called by that name since being with the Mitnicks in Switzerland.

"Who gives a fuck. He can wear what he wants, but I'm not sure I'd advise wearing that to class at this school. Who's Jonny?" Bill asked.

"That's him," Pat said pointing at me. "Like Johnny Mathis, right? Even he couldn't pull off a suit like that. He may have had a velvet voice but no velvet like that!"

"Just let me share with you the immortal words I live by. Good fucks make good babies. Just remember that. Good fucks make good babies. You know who said that?" Bill asked.

Pat looked at me and I looked at Bill. It was obvious to both of us that he was as drunk as we were, if not drunker. He must have had several cocktails after his shift at the tavern.

"Norman Mailer, you motherfuckers. That's who said it," he said, rubbing his chin.

# chapter 16

The Norman Mailer quote troubled me. Was it true? How was it true? How would I know if it was true? I had no experience to prove it or refute it, so I decided to stop probing it for whatever guidance it would yield and concentrate on Plato's dialogues, which, unlike Norman Mailer, had survived millennia of scrutiny. I winced when I read that poets had to be exiled from Plato's Republic because their understanding of the real world was limited to second- or third-hand representations of the "thing itself."

My professor for the great Greek philosophers was Dr. Jasha Klein, a German Jewish refugee named who had fled the Nazis and wound up teaching college students in Maryland. Texts that he had pondered and written about for decades were pawed over by his freshmen students. He attempted to simplify the concepts for us.

When the seminar reached Aristotle's idea of the "unmoved mover" in the *Metaphysics*, the discussion struggled with what he or she must be like. "Stop," Dr. Klein insisted in a heavy German accent that made the letter *w* sound like a *v*. "We are making this far too complicated. Imagine a beautiful woman," he said. "She is the Venus of Botticelli standing naked. But she is not on a clamshell. She is inside that cupboard," he said, pointing with his arthritic index finger toward the large book-filled wardrobe in the corner. "We open the doors. We see her and we cannot help ourselves. We cannot stop from reaching for her. From wanting her. We walk toward her like she is the sun. That is the unmoved mover. It is like desire." He finished speaking, and it seemed like everyone but me looked at the wardrobe as if the idea was breathtakingly clear.

As the class let out and we walked down the stairs, the girl walking next to me, Daphne, asked if I could explain the discussion to her. I had been watching Daphne from the first night because, like me, she almost never spoke in class. I had looked her up in the student directory and knew she was from New York City, but that was all I'd learned about her. She had straight brown bangs that swung in front of her eyes like a cotton curtain. She was tall and bony and dressed in pleated knee-length skirts, thick stockings, and sweaters even though it was still warm out. When she spoke she tilted her head to the side as though a different angle might help her find a better way into the conversation. She had big brown eyes, thick eyebrows, and cheeks that looked as if she were biting them from inside her mouth.

"We learned that desire and the unmoved mover are the same thing," I said. She didn't respond.

"Do you think his theory of the unmoved mover applies to girls?" she asked. I didn't answer her for a minute because I had no idea and wasn't sure what to say.

"Isn't the theory gender-neutral?" I finally asked.

"No, it doesn't work for me, this idea of Venus," she said. "When I think a boy is cute I don't go toward him as if he were the sun. That is a man's idea. I wait and sniff around to see what I can find out about him. Eager lurking, I call it. That way he will happen upon me and think he found me all by himself. Who's the unmoved mover in that case?" she asked in her husky voice.

"I think you should ask Dr. Klein, but I'm not sure he would understand it from a female point of view."

"Never mind," she said. "I'd rather not risk embarrassing myself. I think I can work it out alone."

Instinctively we walked toward the Little Campus together. "My Dad works in advertising," she told me, "and his idea of success, his only idea of success, or the only one he ever mentioned to me, was not to own too many bed frames and mattresses."

"What does that mean? Is he an insomniac?" I asked her. She smiled.

"No, not at all. He nods off and starts snoring all the time. He thinks that beds have lethal plots against us. They lull us into inaction. The day he realized that we lived in an apartment that had four bedrooms and there were mattresses and bed frames in each of them and there were only three of us in the house, he was depressed for weeks. He didn't even go to work."

"That's odd. What do you think they represent to him?" I asked her. "Softness? Complacency? Too much desire? Infirmity?"

"No, that's not it," she said. "I think that they give him a false sense of stability. Like he's become bourgeois and the mattresses are symbols of disinterest in the real, struggling world."

I wondered if our meeting on the stairs was really accidental. Maybe she had been lurking for me. Surely she didn't think I was attractive, did she? My hyperawareness of my weight and size prevented me from believing that anyone might see me as anything but a hardship case, an exercise in pity. When I pictured myself, I dangled from the chin-up bar in the closet, desperately trying to pull myself up one more time.

Daphne, I realized, was the incarnation of the unmoved mover, and I was attracted to her immediately, her voice full of leaf tobacco, the heavy clothing that contrasted with her lively eyes and sideways looks. Attraction was not new to me. I had felt attracted to Ingrid and Natalie too. But with Daphne, with whom I had no contract, implied or otherwise, I had no idea how to bridge the space between us. Her body was isolated and protected by an invisible neutral zone. At first the distance between us seemed trivial, but as soon as I became aware of it, its size was no longer calculable. It had become oceanic.

Where was the simple magnetism that had propelled me toward Natalie? Where was the lust for attention that had consumed me in Madrid? If I could locate and marshal either of those instincts, then I could urge myself toward Daphne. In my mind I reached for her, but my arm didn't move. My body was the enemy of my mind.

"Where did you go to school before this?" she asked.

"Lots of places. What about you?" I asked her.

"I went to the same Manhattan school for twelve years. They didn't believe me when I said I wanted to come here," she said. She sat across from me in the same booth where Pat had sat drinking himself into oblivion. Her high forehead was like a reflector. Her hand was on the table, but I couldn't reach for it. I grabbed my thigh through my pocket and squeezed it, hoping that the pressure would snap me out of my paralysis.

"Where did they think you should go?" I asked, while the din of arguments against myself became increasingly loud and hectic.

"Wellesley or Smith or somewhere like that. I didn't want one of those old-fashioned places. This is different, off to the side. I found it on my own. They'd heard of it at my school, but no one they knew had ever actually gone here before," she said.

I could barely hear what she was saying over the voice inside me that shouted at me to reach for her. I nodded. We finished our drink and walked back to campus. She sat down on one of the stone benches overlooking the lower grounds of the campus, and I sat next to her. Where was I supposed to put my hands? She fiddled with her hair, and I caught her peeking at me through its scrim. My leg started to jiggle and I couldn't make it stop.

She stood up abruptly, as if her patience had come to an end. "I have to go," she said. Should I kiss her on the cheek? Shake hands? The cavalcade of questions overwhelmed me.

"Okay," was all I could manage to say. We didn't hug or even kiss each other politely on the cheek as I had learned to do with the girls at École Nouvelle. She walked away in her long-legged gait, as though her limbs outpaced her torso. I headed back to my dorm room excoriating myself for my reticence. At least I could have looked her in the eye as Dad had taught me, the minimum of human connection.

After that night, Daphne and I spent hours together talking, debating, and arguing, and yet I still couldn't reach across the void to her. She looked at me in a wounded way as if there were something wrong with me, something missing, while concluding that this must mean that there was something wrong with her, too. I had a hunch that she blamed herself. Or did she assume that we were merely friends? Around her, I grew conscious of my breathing. My throat felt parched when I tried to swallow. A strange sensitivity flared in my fingers and toes. At first it was a minor symptom, and then it distracted me from her. Even in conversation I was unable to sound natural, not to mention intimate. An uncomfortable silence filled the gulf between us.

One afternoon sitting in her room she said gently, "You don't have to be so nervous around me, you know?" She inched closer to where I was sitting on the floor and broke through the neutral space between us. She kissed me on the lips in a lunge and pushed her tongue inside my mouth. Only Natalie and Marco had kissed me on the lips before. This was almost as shocking and invasive as if she had reached inside my body and stolen my composure, my most private possession. Ingrid and Natalie hadn't dared do that. They hadn't come close. I was startled, and jerked away from her. Then she edged closer to me again and yanked me toward her and kissed me again.

"Are you afraid of me?" she asked. "Obviously you are, but why?"

"I don't know," I said, and looked away. I imagined my mother sitting at the end of my bed as she assessed my body. I was frozen by the intensity of her stare. Daphne's questions were meant with kindness, but I felt assaulted by them, as though any one of them might have a trick in it.

"I don't want to hurt you, you know. I like you. I want to know you better," she said.

"Maybe that's what I'm afraid of," I said. "Maybe I can't." She reached for me again and put her hand inside my shirt. It felt cool and smooth as a river stone, and I shivered.

"You can touch me, Jonathan, if you want. I would like that," she said. But even with permission, I couldn't force my hand toward her. I could be touched, but I couldn't reach out to touch her. My fingers felt tingly, as if they were being given instructions in a language they hadn't been taught. With supreme effort, I put my hand on her shoulder. It felt superfluous there, and insincere.

"Don't you think I'm pretty?" she asked me, and swung her hair to the side. Her eyes were dark and tantalizing, flashing through her fringe at an obtuse angle.

"Yes," I said. "I think you are, Daphne." She lifted her heavy black sweater over her head and pulled her arms through the sleeves. She turned her bra around and unhooked it. Then she looked at me.

"Don't you want to touch my skin, Jonathan? Are you going to make me undress myself?" I thought about the question and forced myself toward her. I wanted to confess to her why I couldn't speak, but I couldn't form the words.

"I want to but ..." I muttered.

"It's not so hard," she said. She took my hand and put it on her side before moving it to her breast. I could barely feel her skin. My hand was cold. Her ribs felt as flat as my own did, and bunched up against her waist.

Daphne did everything for me. She unbuttoned my shirt and held it while I pulled my hands out. I unbuckled my belt, but she held on to me as I stepped out of my pants. When I was naked I crossed my arms and wrapped them around my sides. She spoke in a dreamy monologue. Unlike Ingrid and Natalie, she was unfocused. She shooed flies away and batted down the dust motes that were spotlit by the late sun. She talked casually and comfortably about anything, as if there were nothing illicit between us—even my odd behavior. My silence was a disease that spread from my brain through my body. It was a state of being. Like skinniness.

We made love deliberately and awkwardly under the paisley scarves that hung like flags from the cement-block ceiling. She was too lanky for me, I thought. Her bones stuck out. She was jagged. There was too much of her for me to manage with her long legs and jutting hips, her furtive glances, her ideas about boys and how to maneuver them, the unmoved mover and her father with his surplus of mattresses and that school she'd gone to for all those years. There was too much life to put my arms around. My arms weren't long enough. Then I realized that she was not too big for me; I was too small for her. My body couldn't accommodate her, and there was not enough room for her whole person in my thoughts, yet she appeared not to notice my deficiency.

As I lay next to her on my side, she rested her hand on my hip and rubbed my back absentmindedly. Her generosity overwhelmed me. I knew I had to speak. I had to be thankful or grateful or touch her hair gently, but all I could do was steel myself for something painful, as if I were a child again in the doctor's waiting room who knew he was scheduled for a shot. The silence lengthened and sagged. It pressed outward against the wall and windows like a low-pressure system. I wanted to disappear, but I was still there, left behind.

Compared with Ingrid and especially Natalie, Daphne seemed plain. She didn't tease her hair or wear mascara. There was no idle flattery. Without those over-seductive attributes, she seemed feature-less. I wanted love to feel shared, adventuresome, and joyous yet unique to me. I imagined it filling me and providing me with the gravity that I lacked. That love would knit the loose skein of muscles and nerves together and tighten them enough to make me stand taller. I would swell inside my skin and feel that newfound power. But when Daphne offered something like that to me in a natural way, I couldn't recognize it for what I wanted. The expression of normal desire made me want to flee from her or from myself.

"I think I have to go," I managed.

"Why? You can't go now," she said, imploring. "Please stay with me."

"No, I have to leave. I can't stay. It's not your fault." I stood up from the mattress that she had moved from the bed frame to the floor. I sat on the wooden chair and put my pants on in a trance. I told myself to keep moving. Don't stop or you'll collapse. She watched me, looking hurt and bewildered. When I was dressed and put my jacket on I looked at her and thought I was going to tumble apart, but instead I forced myself through the door.

Walking back along the path to my dorm, I felt overwhelmed by all of the things I had failed to do and say. I was not human. I was not grateful for her kindness and her gentleness. My self-censorship was agitated, not attentive or kind. If I felt any warmth for her, I could not express it or even locate it. The weight of my inadequacy was a burden that pressed down on me so forcefully that I could barely lift my feet.

When I opened the door to my room, I went straight to my bed and lay down with my coat on. I stretched my arms back to the window behind me. On the ledge were many of the upcoming books from the syllabus. I picked out the first one my hand found and propped it up on my chest. It was the Bible. I had only read small sections before, so I opened it at random. The Psalms. I ran my finger down the seventeen entries of the first chapter and stopped arbitrarily at number fourteen, which read, "My beloved is unto me as a cluster of henna in the vineyards of En-Gedi." The tenderness in these lines seemed so absent in me that the book slipped out of my hands.

My father had tried to help transform me into a man, his idea of a man, but the man that I had become seemed to be missing vital emotional components. I couldn't speak directly. I didn't know how to express the simplest feeling. Nor could I feel any emotion inside me. Instead there was a mass of doubt and theory that I couldn't see through. Dad had introduced me to sex, but sex that was split off from emotion, pleasurable but thin. I was a stunted boy. I wanted to force myself to go back to Daphne's room and explain this to her and tell her how it had happened, but I knew I couldn't.

When we saw each other a few days later she searched my eyes for an answer that would explain my abrupt departure. Neither of us said anything besides hello. She studied my face, hoping that what-ever obstacle had restrained me might suddenly have dissolved. But I was the same, lost inside myself. In my fantasy of manhood, I dreamed of putting my arms around her and holding her close to me, comforting her and feeling her confidence in me. Softly, I said, "Good-bye" when we parted. That was as close as I could come.

A few days later we ran into each other again. "Will you walk with me back to my room?" she asked. I agreed, reluctantly. "I didn't want that much from you. Did I? Why did you run away? Why can't you say something to me? What did I do to you?" she asked. One question by itself, the same one as before, was difficult for me. In a bunch they overwhelmed me. She stared at me, and her forehead knotted angrily until it looked like she might burst. I didn't think she was going to hurt me, but I could feel how hurt she was and how badly she wanted an explanation. There was only one thing to do. I turned and walked away as quickly as I could.

In the days that followed, I kept as much distance from Daphne as I could, which was difficult because the campus was small and we were in the same class. If I saw her coming toward me, I took a quick turn to avoid her. Her friends scowled at me when we passed, as if I were a monster. Daphne was the embodiment of all of my gaps, a reminder that I was small and incapable, a reinforcement of every criticism I had ever been given about myself. As much effort as I spent dodging her, the feelings that she provoked swamped me. My body felt severed from itself, as though my skin was a paper bag that contained a jumble of random, unrelated parts. Daphne was proof that my father's judgments were accurate.

# chapter 17

B ill was sitting in the corner of Little Campus when I walked in. We had agreed to meet there for a beer. He was wearing his houndstooth jacket and pink Brooks Brothers shirt, his uniform on the nights he didn't have to put on the white butcher's apron and sturdy waitering shoes for his shift at Middleton Tavern. Pat was there too and barely looked up when I sat down.

"Hey, Sport," Pat mumbled.

Something felt amiss. Bill was hunched over the small table, smoking and coughing and gulping his drink at the same time. "I talked to Daphne yesterday. What did you do to that poor girl?" he asked, staring into me. "She told me she wants to drop out of school. Was that what you had in mind? To never speak to her again? To never explain yourself, just walk away and say nothing? To give her the silent treatment? How could you do that? What am I supposed to tell her? That's not what a man does."

"What *does* a man do, Bill?" I asked facetiously.

"A man blames himself for whatever went wrong and tells her that she's wonderful. Whether she is or she isn't, it doesn't matter. He says it's his fault, not hers. He doesn't clam up like that."

"Why did she ask you? Since when did she want your opinion?" I asked him. There was a dead weight in the pit of my stomach. I didn't know how to respond, so I sat quietly and let the humiliation crash over me.

"Well, she knows I'm your friend and that you might have confided to me what your reasons were. So tell me what happened. I just want to understand it for myself. I won't repeat it to her."

I didn't want to be pressed to give answers to behavior I could barely understand myself. It was bitter enough to think about how I'd acted without dissecting it with my friends. Did I have to go back into the past and tell them the whole story? And even if I did, was it an excuse, a rationalization for what I hadn't been able to master? The more questions I asked myself, the more self-righteous I became. I looked at my watch. It was almost time for dinner. Any nondescript meal would be better than an interrogation. Bill kept staring at me. Pat watched the foam float on the surface of his beer, and the silence lingered.

"I was afraid," I admitted. "Afraid of her asking me too much that I didn't want to tell her about. I didn't want her to know how much I couldn't say to her, so I thought it was better to say nothing. Keep it to myself. She wanted to know too much. That's all I can tell you."

"Hold on," Pat said. "What are we talking about? If she wanted you to tell her stuff you didn't want to talk about, you were right to give her the cold shoulder. Buck up, Sport. It's not that complicated. Just because she asks doesn't mean you have to spill the beans."

"I don't want to talk about it even with my friends." I had a strong urge to leave. Except for during the worst moments with Daphne, I rarely thought about Dad's decision to introduce me to Ingrid and Natalie. But on the few occasions when I did, it no longer seemed like a carefree adventure. It had lost its power to thrill and to distract potential tormentors. Maturity had converted the memory of it into shame, the shame that needed my father to intervene and to direct me in my search for love rather than letting me stumble into it like any other adolescent. The shame that said that he didn't think I had the ability to find it on my own or at least the version of it that he wanted for me. I preferred running away to sharing that information.

"Don't leave, Jon. We're your friends. You don't have to tell us anything you don't want to. I'm sorry. I wasn't trying to lecture you. She asked me, and I wanted to know what your side of the story was. That's all. But we don't have to know anything you don't want to tell us." Bill said, his voice wavering. He gave me a look to say that he meant it with the utmost sincerity.

But no matter what his tone was, I didn't want to hear any more questions or speculations or apologies. Even sympathy couldn't have kept me there. I stood up and left the two of them to wonder at what had happened to me. Disappearing was the only action that could salvage my dignity.

When I got back to my room, Roger, my roommate, was studying at his desk. The overhead light was off, and his Greek textbook was open, lit only by a small lamp. He was copying some words into a notebook. I nodded as I entered. We were cordial at best during the few times we were together in the room and both of us were awake.

I lay down on my bed and hoped he would say or do something. He sat still, and his writing hand moved deliberately across the paper. He was quiet and diligent and kept mostly to himself. Roger was from a rural town in Virginia where his family had lived for hundreds of years. His parents hadn't come to drop him off as mine had. He had appeared as though out of nowhere.

At that moment Roger's total indifference was appealing. I sat down at my desk and looked out of my window. In the near dark I could see the spire of St. Anne's Church in the nearby circle poking at the sky. Then I turned to the row of books leaning against the window. I pulled out the *Collected Poems of T. S. Eliot*. I opened it to "The Love Song of J. Alfred Prufrock," my first and favorite Eliot poem, and read it to myself. I knew many of the lines by heart. It was the first poem I had ever actually read on a page. When the seventh-grade teacher in my English class at Adams Academy had asked what the tone of the poem was I raised my hand unexpectedly and gave a rambling answer about dislocation and regret. The teacher listened to me with a level of interest I wasn't used to. When I finished he thanked me in a way that made me feel as if I had never been thanked for anything before that moment. As I reread the poem, I remembered how big an impression it had made on me the first time I read it, when the idea of preparing a face to meet other faces was novel. Before it had become second nature.

"Have you eaten yet, Roger?" I asked.

Roger closed his textbook and turned around in his chair to look at me, surprised that I had broken our silence. He wasn't used to us speaking to each other. Now his natural quiet made him appear dignified. His neutrality and lack of curiosity was a blessing. I suggested we go to the dining hall, and without a word he turned off his lamp, got his hunter's coat from the closet, and then stood patiently by the door.

We walked across the dark campus together. The lamps along the way lit up the brick paths. The giant oak trees rustled over our heads. As we approached the building, the noise of a hundred kids laughing and talking made a low rumble like an avalanche that had been triggered way up in the highest mountain chute. A rumble that hadn't yet turned into a roar.

The dining room was a tableau of animated eighteen- and nineteen-year-olds. Most of the juniors and seniors had already moved off campus. They sat in familiar groupings. In the far corner I could see the one I usually sat with, including Bill and Pat. Daphne was there, sitting next to Bill. Her head was thrown back in laughter, and her lank hair fell straight down between her shoulder blades. Bill's hand was resting on her lower back, and he was leaning toward her as though they were sharing a confidence. So that was how he was consoling her, explaining me to her, passing off my actions as those of a juvenile who hadn't learned yet what it meant to be human. Bill's solace had been converted to tenderness, and tenderness had turned into intimacy.

I followed Roger to the food line, and when I reached the end I took my tray to the opposite side of the dining room. Roger and I ate without speaking or looking up.

I swallowed without tasting. The misery of Bill's betrayal and the exposure of my immaturity stupefied me, and the only relief I could think of was going home. Not finishing the cafeteria food. I felt like excusing myself to Roger, packing up a few things, and taking the bus to New York City that night. Even if I missed a few classes, at least when I came back I would have a chance to return whole. I wanted to spend a week in my room with the door closed. I could study without intrusions, and that would give me the chance to make the necessary inner adjustments.

# chapter 18

Entering my house, I noticed a distinct aroma. Instead of the traditional cooking smells coming from the kitchen, there was an exotic Indian scent in the air, like sandalwood or patchouli. It didn't take me long to realize that it was incense, the smoke leaking from beneath the closed library doors at the end of the front hallway and getting sucked out through the front door, which I had just opened. I had smelled incense before, in hippie shops on St. Mark's Place that Tim I had visited on the weekends—but I never expected the smell to take over the home I had grown up in. I couldn't say that I hadn't been warned.

Danny had picked up the telephone when I called the night before. He was only twelve, and it struck me that he would be the perfect messenger to pass along the announcement that I was coming home for a few days. Speaking with him would spare me the inconvenience of justifying why I was leaving school before the week was over. Before hanging up he had told me be prepared: "Aliens have landed in our house." When I asked who they were, he said, "You'll see. I don't want to spoil the surprise."

Mom appeared, throwing her arms around my neck. Resting her cheek against mine for a brief moment, she lifted her index finger to her lips to silence me before I could say a single word. She took me by the hand and led me to the back hall toward the kitchen.

"Sorry, darling. I didn't mean to shush you, but I don't want to disturb Adnan. He's meditating in the library," she said.

"Who's Adnan?"

"He's our Sufi friend. He's staying with us for a little while, and we are lucky and honored that he's here. He wants to teach us, and we're eager to learn from him." My mother sounded as if she had been abducted by a religious cult and reprogrammed. She hadn't even said hello or What are you doing here?

"You are? Where did you meet him?"

"Dad and I met him a month ago at a retreat in California. It's called Esalen. In Big Sur. It's filled with teachers and gurus. Students from all over the world. It was wonderful. There was so much knowledge there. So many wise men and women to listen to, so Dad thought we should offer one of them a place to stay for a while. I hope you don't mind, but we put him in your cottage."

During previous summers when Tim and I came home from school, Mom let us barricade ourselves in a one-bedroom cabin that was a few hundred yards from the main house beyond the swimming pool. To transform it from its Yankee origins of hooked rugs and uncomfortable wooden furniture, to possess it and make the cottage ours, Tim and I lugged our albums and stereo system over. On humid summer nights, we cranked the volume up as loud as we could, knowing that the noise would only be heard by moths and fireflies. Stoned, we played air guitar to our favorite solos. It was our private outbuilding. Even though it was late autumn, I was counting on staying there with my albums and stereo for company.

There was no arguing about this, as the cottage had already been loaned to Adnan. I convinced myself that it would be better to be in the main house with Danny anyway. Isolation wouldn't help me focus.

I didn't hear Danny enter and didn't notice at first that he had crept in behind me. He grabbed me around the waist and rested his shaggy head against my back. He hadn't grown much beyond his boyhood height, and that was as close as he could get to giving me a brotherly hug. Sinbad came in behind him and slobbered against the legs of my jeans.

"There's something fishy about Adnan," Danny said, having overheard Mom's description of him. "For instance, you'd think that if he was a real Sufi master, he would know how to levitate, but he says he doesn't do that. What's the use of being a master, then? Master of what? That's the only thing I want to learn. Wouldn't it be cool to be able to hover in the air?"

"How many times have I told you that he doesn't come from that part of the sect. He's not one of the mystics," Mom said in exasperation.

Danny was an expert at asking the question that got under her skin, questions he had asked many times before and already knew the answer to.

Danny pulled me out the door and up the back stairs. It felt as though I hadn't been in his bedroom in years, and yet it was exactly the same as it had been before I left for Switzerland. The giant tortoise shell hung on the wall over his bed, as did the lithograph of bear paws. Danny hadn't changed. He was still more at ease with animals and the outdoors than with his parents and the rest of the household. Even the stomp mat on the floor of the closet, which Mom and Dad had bought to try to cure him of his tantrums, remained in its place. He and I had spent many evenings in there as I encouraged him to keep pounding his small brown lace-up shoes into the plastic mat that, helpfully, bore the outline of red feet so the penitent would know exactly where to stamp. At the end of every session he emerged exhausted though rarely repentant.

"I can tell you enjoy needling him. Who is this guy?" I asked him, sitting in his child-sized red armchair.

"He's their guru. I can't stand him. We all hate him except Mom and Dad. At dinner he gives us his teachings and makes us hold hands and bow our heads. You'll see. Holding hands is the worst!"

The dinner bell rang. Dad stood in the entry. I barely recognized him. He had a full salt-and-pepper beard that hid the bottom half of his face, and he wasn't wearing a suit or tie. He beamed at me, as if all the slyness and cynicism had been drained from his eyes. The familiar expressions—the sideways smile, the mouth tic, the double take, the slow panning across the supplicant's face—had been replaced by a blankly blissful countenance. He stared at me with childlike wonder, as though he was seeing the real me for the first time.

"What a nice surprise!" he exclaimed, and embraced me. I regarded him suspiciously. He extracted the *Wall Street Journal* from his briefcase and handed it to me as if it were a spiritual offering.

"What are you doing home?"

"I needed some time to regroup, Dad. Let's say I'm adjusting slowly to college and had to step back for a few days."

"All right with me, but do me a favor, please. Be nice to our guest. Adnan is a holy man, and it is a privilege to have him with us. He's not used to American teenagers and our kind of kidding around, so let's keep it on the Q.T. in front of him, okay?"

As he was speaking to me I heard the library doors open and felt someone approaching from behind. Before I could turn around, I felt a heavy paw on my shoulder.

"Adnan, this is Jonathan, our eldest," Dad said. In front of me, a little too close, I saw a radiant brown face staring at me without blinking. He wore a sweeping white toga-like gown and sandals with white socks. Strands of wooden beads were wrapped around his wrists. He smiled as though no news, no matter how catastrophic, could puncture his serenity.

"What a pleasure to meet the scholar of the family. Your parents are so proud of your studies," he said. This came as a surprise to me. Except for my French fluency, I had never had any sense of their pride in my academic ability. Clearly, his first instinct was to flatter me, not realizing how much its hollowness annoyed me.

We swept into the dining room. A reverent, alien hush enveloped us as we served ourselves from the platter that was passed by Irene, the compact Portuguese cook who had replaced Marianita when she returned to her family in Ecuador. The appearance of the food was indistinct, a mush of lentils and vegetables that might have been nutritious but also looked tasteless. Adnan took a small spoonful on his plate and picked quietly at it. The loud, rambunctious dinner-table rituals of years past were replaced by a cautious, respectful silence. Danny rummaged through the vegetable heap on his plate, no doubt seeking a nugget of real flavor buried inside the sludge. I pushed the indifferent food around my plate, eating as little as possible. In this new spiritual environment, Dad didn't notice or seem to care how little I ate. The only sound was the silverware jousting with the plates.

It was a solemn, almost mournful meal until Adnan began to hold forth.

"In our religion the archetypes are related: the wise man, the fakir, the king. These are Sufis but not Sufism itself. Sufism is what binds us.

We are poets, scholars, merchants. A Sufi who becomes a millionaire like your father is not a millionaire first. He is a Sufi first." I turned to look at Dad. He was grinning, pleased with the new designation.

"You may see your father as a rich man. Society may see him as a millionaire, but to me he is a Sufi." I looked at Dad basking in Adnan's tribute and tried to suppress my amazement at the change in him. His derision had melted into a spiritual puddle. As much as I wanted to believe it, I was skeptical that such a big change could happen so suddenly.

"So for Sufis, Sufism always comes first?" Mom asked, bright-eyed and eager.

"For us, money and mysticism are inseparable," he said. Mom nodded as if she understood, but I wondered if she didn't find the braiding of wealth and spirituality difficult to swallow. She always railed at us when we wanted to buy anything on Sunday, whether the stores were open or not. "Can't we have one noncommercial day out of seven?" she would plead.

"But what about Jesus throwing the money changers out of the temple? Wouldn't your priests do the same thing Jesus did?" I finally interjected.

"What do you mean?" Adnan asked.

"The New Testament says that Jesus threw the traders out of the temple. They did not belong in his place of worship or his religion. In Matthew. He said they defaced his faith, but you say that they are as holy as you are, so it seems to me that it has to be one or the other. Both can't be right. The traders and the usurers can't be scorned in one religion and accepted in another. All religions share the belief that God's love can't be bought. So someone must be wrong. Unless you accommodate them, accept their money and their hospitality, and then reject them later."

"That's not what Adnan said, Jon," Dad said.

"I know that's not what he said, but that's what he means. He will take what he wants from you and call you holy while he lives in your house. Would he find you as holy if he wasn't receiving the benefits of your hospitality?" I could feel the bile rise in my chest and scorch the bottom of my throat like reflux. I closed my eyes in an attempt to block Adnan out. Then I pictured a righteous Christ-like figure, a long bearded man in robes turning over the traders' makeshift tables as silver coins scattered across the floor. I was his fellow crusader, his acolyte, remonstrating with the malefactors and shoving them down the temple stairs. I liked imagining myself as a biblical figure if only to compensate for my transgressions against Daphne. It was my mistreatment of her that had led to my being disrespectful in my own home.

"Careful," Dad said, glaring at me. "Adnan is our guest."

"I know he is our guest, but that doesn't mean that I have to agree with whatever he says, do I? What he says sounds like patter. I know what you'd really call it if we were talking alone. And why is he more right than a rabbi or a priest? Because he's from India? At least one of them comes from our spiritual traditions!"

"Sufism is an ancient religion, Jonathan. We don't make the types of distinctions that you are making. Those aren't important to us."

The antique wood of Mom and Dad's chairs squeaked. They looked at each other and each glanced at me with a vague sense of concern, as if I had come down with a highly contagious disease. Dad stroked his beard, a delaying gesture I hadn't seen before.

"Let him ask his question again, Arnold," Adnan said.

"Never mind. I don't want to say anything else. Go on. It doesn't matter. Pretend I'm not here and never said a word."

Adnan started speaking again, but I ignored him. I didn't really want to hear any more. Instead, I hoped that Mom or Dad might ask me, provoked by some parental instinct, if everything was all right; might notice that something was amiss and listen as I explained the misery I had caused Daphne and myself.

After dinner, Dad took me by the arm and pulled me aside. He sat me down in the library where Adnan had been chanting and burning incense and closed the doors behind him. The room still reeked of incense. I looked around and noticed the rows of books that stood out from the wall, surprised at how many I could recognize by the thin strip of color and design on their spines.

"What the hell is wrong with you? You don't look well. Your clothes don't fit you. Your body is out of kilter. You don't have to agree with what Adnan says, but you could be a little less confrontational about it. You used to be such a gentle boy. What happened?" he asked, and searched my face for a clue to where my sweetness had fled. He reached his mangled right hand toward me. I thought for one magical second that he was going to pat me on the head or let it rest on my shoulder sympathetically. A hug would have overwhelmed me. If I had requested it, I was sure he'd say that wasn't what men did or not our kind of men anyway. Instead, he stuck his twisted index finger in the air.

"Hold on, it's coming into focus. I know who to send you to. This guy is brilliant. You are out of balance. That's obvious. Even I can see it, and I'm no expert. What is that school doing to you? It seems like it's fouled you up in the head. I can tell your mother is worried about you, too. Is there something wrong with you that you'd like to share with me?"

"I wasn't expecting to find a stranger living in our house," I said, afraid to tell him the truth. "There's nothing wrong with me. I'm not sick. I was just curious what he'd say if I brought that Bible passage up. I didn't call him bad names like apostate or lemming."

I punished myself for censoring what was really preoccupying me, but I realized then that I wasn't any more able to confide in him than I was in Daphne. Nor would I be able to trust him with how I had behaved toward her because he was as much to blame for my behavior as I was.

"Okay, but I'm going to make an appointment for you anyway. Something or someone has made you toxic, and I want to help you figure it out. Not watch it happen. You remember what I say, don't you?"

I wasn't sure which stock phrase he had in mind that would fit the situation.

"Not to decide is to decide." He had passed on this pronouncement to me and Tim countless times, and yet it still didn't quite add up for me. I wasn't sure what not deciding decided. Or maybe that was the point of it. It decided nothing. You were in the same lousy position you had always been in.

"It's called Rolfing. It's a form of radical massage. Matthew really knows how to get into your muscles and joints and break through your knots. But be prepared. It's not a feel-good massage. It's a lot more strenuous than that. I think it'd be perfect for you. Shake you up. Get you out of your head. I'll set it up for you tomorrow. I assume you're staying that long. Since when do you quote the Bible, by the way?"

The question dangled in the air unanswered.

# chapter 19

R iding the elevator up to Dad's office, I felt nervous, conned, and deflected at the same time. Although I had been unable to tell him what was really on my mind, he had sensed there was a problem and shifted it from his shoulders to the hands of an anonymous bodyworker. Echoes of his previous interventions came to mind as I walked down the hallway. Matthew, it seemed, was merely the New Age massage substitute for Natalie and Ingrid.

"Is this legitimate massage, Dad?" I asked as soon as I closed the door behind me. "Or is it code for something else?"

"What are you asking me?" he answered indignantly. "Are you suggesting that I'm sending you to another girl? If so, you couldn't be more mistaken. No more girls for you. You're cured of that, but you have to admit it got you off the dime?" I didn't know how to respond to his obnoxious comment.

"You're on your own with girls now," he continued.

"Well, if I'm cured, then what's the Rolfing for?"

"It's a different problem area that obviously needs attention. Rolfing is a serious medical practice. You are lucky that I can afford to send you to Matthew. He will unlock you. Like I said, you're toxic. A crumpled old man in a kid's body. What a shame! Why are you so suspicious of everything? Couldn't you just trust me for once?"

I felt ungrateful suddenly ashamed of my previous ingratitude. I stood silently in his hushed, carpeted office. Big decisions happened here, I thought to myself as I looked around the room. Decisions that could affect me and many other people. It was right for him to be upset with me. He was trying to fortify me in the only way he knew, no matter how misguided it appeared to me. I went over and took the piece of paper with Matthew's address on it from his hand.

At the Upper West Side apartment where I was to receive the final adjustment, a gangly young man greeted me. He seemed barely older than I was. His T-shirt and loose drawstring pants barely disguised how thin he was. The whiskers on his sunken cheeks were wispy and grew in splotches. The room had almost no furniture, just a thin pad on the floor and a rickety chair. Some light slanted in through the speckled bamboo blinds that looked as though they came from Chinatown.

"Hi, Jon. Your Dad told me a little about you. He said you were misaligned and closed down emotionally. Would you agree with that diagnosis?" he asked. Was this how he had described me to a stranger? I was both stunned and stumped, not wanting to concede anything, no matter how accurate it was.

"That's his opinion," I said, and shrugged. "Maybe he's right. I'm not sure, and I'm not sure I want to be here, either."

"If you don't think this will help you, we don't have to start," he said. "But I can tell from a quick look at you that your body is out of balance. Your left arm is a little longer than your right, and that leads me to believe that your shoulder is holding on to the muscles and locking the arm up inside the socket. Okay, let's see what we can do. Take your clothes off except for your underwear," Matthew said.

I undressed it in slow motion, as if I were cooperating and resisting at the same time. Matthew began by rubbing my shoulders and arms softly, gently pulling, lengthening, and testing the muscles. For a moment I relaxed, but seconds later I understood why Dad had used the term "radical." Matthew dug his elbow so deeply into my armpit that, as I flinched in response, I thought I was going to faint from the pain or throw up. Gripping my jaw from underneath with both hands and pulling up on it, he put his foot on the shoulder that he claimed was jammed. I thought I heard a crack that sounded exactly like my leg snapping on the ski slope. Instinctively, my whole body became rigid. A moment later I'd wriggled free and leapt up. "What the hell are you doing to me?"

"Be calm, be calm. This is what I *do*. It's an intervention. That's what you need. It is so obvious to me. Didn't your father explain that to you? There is no release without pain, my friend. That's the way it is, so lie back down on the mat. You'll feel much better when I'm done. I think most of the problem is in your neck, so that's where I want to concentrate."

I refused to look at him and pretended he was no longer in the room. In a rage that blurred the blinds, the chair, the Indian-style prints on the wall, and the scrawny figure in front of me, I put my clothes on as best I could.

"You're really not giving this a chance," Matthew said.

Fumbling, I tied my sneakers and cinched my belt. "Good," I said with all of the fury I could muster. On the way out I slammed his door so hard, it sounded like an explosion. I jumped down the stairs three at a time, as if I had been shot from a cannon. I felt loose, untangled, and free of gravity. When I reached the sidewalk, the sun bathed me in warmth. I felt happy and proud of myself for reacting against this latest assault, my accusers and shamers fading into an indistinguishable, irrelevant mass.

The feeling stayed with me during the train ride home, when I walked in the front door and went up to my room. I had never stood up for myself so vehemently before, and I could feel the joyous, rippling effects surge through me. The power made my body lengthen as if I were one of the wooden Italian marionettes that Mom had brought home for us as souvenirs. They had fascinated me as a child, how malleable their wooden bodies were compared with mine. Now I had yanked the strings on my own body, realizing my power to do so for the first time. My shoulders unhunched, and my spine elongated. I was two or three inches taller suddenly. My chin lifted off my chest. My legs felt muscled and long. I plopped down on the orange-and-brown bean bag chair and stretched my new limbs out. Something deep and fundamental had changed in me.

"What's wrong with you?" Danny asked, sitting down next to me. "Why are you smiling like that? By the way, Teddy and Svetlana are here. Wait until you meet them. They're nuts. They come up on the weekends a lot and sit with us at every meal."

That night I decided to eat dinner alone in my room. Even with the memories of old intrusions it felt like a sanctuary. The pull-up bar was still wedged into the closet doorway. Our bunk beds were still snug against the wall. I could lie down on the orange rug and listen to music as loud as I wanted without disturbing anyone. After my performance at dinner the previous night, neither parent asked about my absence.

Danny came back up after dinner. "It's safe to come downstairs if you want to. They're holed up in the library. The doors are closed, but we can sneak around the back and spy on them. Come on."

"I don't want to watch them, Danny. Let's just leave them alone."

"Please. Don't make me go by myself. Come on. It'll be fun. You have to watch with me. You have to."

We went downstairs together and out the big front door. It was dark already. The moon was out and almost full. We snuck along the wall behind the bushes. From the outside, the house appeared mammoth and majestic. The metal birdcages that held the doves that Mom had been collecting flashed white in the twilight. Even in my bedroom I could hear them coo all night as if they didn't know they were captives in our house, or maybe they cooed because they knew they were caged and they were more comfortable being fed than forced to hunt for their food in the wild. Their consoling, haunting calls to each other came, went, and returned in my thoughts on a continuous loop. Even at school, waking up in my dorm room in the middle of the night or in geometry class, I thought I could hear them.

We hugged the perimeter of the house and positioned ourselves behind the bush that was next to the wall of windows. Mom and Dad were giggling with the two strangers Danny identified as Teddy and Svetlana. They were passing a lit joint back and forth, sitting in the pit, as we named the spot where we watched television on the weekends. They sat across from one another on facing couches. Adnan slumped in the bay window, looking forlorn and aloof. His white gown looked like a plain bedsheet. The wall sconces lit their faces from the side. Teddy, was big and scruffy and wearing a leather jacket, and he sat so close to Mom that their legs were touching. His burly arm hung over Mom's small shoulders in an intimate way. At some joke we couldn't hear, Mom laughed and threw her head back, snuggling into Teddy's shoulder. He pulled her toward him. Svetlana sat very close to Dad and jerked her peroxide-blond hairdo up abruptly and made a phony shocked face at him in a saucy way, as if he had pinched her bottom when she wasn't looking. The smell of pot smoke seeped toward us through the open windows.

"What do you think they're laughing at? "Danny asked me. "Or is everything funny?"

"They're high as kites," I said. "Look at them."

In the background, the doves called out and other doves answered them. It was hard not to interpret their cries to one another as cries of longing, of not wanting to be apart, and they kept calling because it was their deepest form of consolation. Mom and Dad looked like they were full of longing too, and not for each other. I was filled with disgust. Unlike Danny, I could see clearly what was happening and I couldn't stand to watch any more of it. I took off running and felt sick to my stomach.

The next morning at breakfast I could feel a different strength in me. It wasn't the physical one my father had been pushing relentlessly. It was a solidity that I didn't recognize. My parents and their friends looked sheepish. Even Adnan, who had only been an observer of the previous night's scene, lost in his thoughts and elevated above them, seemed chastened. As I slipped into my chair, Dad introduced me to Teddy and Svetlana, who were wearing the same clothes as they had the night before.

"This is my eldest son, Jonathan," Dad said lamely. "He's the one I told you about who was studying in Switzerland and learned to speak French fluently. Jon," he said, looking at me. "Would you say a few words in French for us? It's been so long since I heard you speak the language. I really miss it." I gave him a disgruntled look.

"What am I supposed to talk about?"

"Whatever you want. Just make something up."

For a few seconds I thought about refusing, and then, realizing I could say anything because no one would understand me, I complied:

"Voici, mon père. Il est bête comme ses pieds. Macaque. Il pense que je vais vous parler en français parce qu'il me le demande. Quel espèce de con. Qui êtes-vous et qu'est-ce que vous foutez ici?" Here is my father, I had said. He is as dumb as his shoes. He thinks that I am going to speak to you in French just because he asked me to. What an idiot! Who are you people, and what the fuck are you doing in our house?

I pronounced the string of insults in a flat tone of voice to not betray myself. Neither he nor Mom nor any of the guests around the table reacted. Dad seemed delighted by my authentic accent, the mellifluous sound of the language, and turned to his guests, who smiled back. After the meal, Dad took me aside. He was upset, but it wasn't about the French. "Matthew called and told me what happened. Why did you do that? I was only trying to help you!"

"Please, don't try to help me anymore, Dad. I don't want it. I want to figure it out for myself."

"Any father would do what I did. It's an instinct. You can't control instincts. Especially paternal ones. Wait until you have kids and you're a father. You'll see."

He spoke sincerely, but his warning was meaningless. I barely thought of myself as an adult, let alone understanding what it meant to be a father.

"Dad, if I was in pain, I could understand your taking me to the doctor. But I was never in any physical pain. You manufactured this whole diagnosis. You've been trying to fix me and improve me since I was eleven. You have to stop. And you're forgetting one very important thing."

"What's that?"

"This is my body, not yours. We aren't the same person, and besides, there's nothing wrong with it. It is what it is. And there never was anything wrong with it. You got carried away. You should have fixed yourself, not me."

The words felt like they were coming from someone else's mouth. He looked over at me glumly, perhaps hoping that I would disown them as soon as I came to my senses. But we both knew that this time

I wouldn't. His beard turned darker where his cheeks creased. I had never seen him so sad, so chastened.

When I was eleven years old standing next to him at the sink as he shaved, I believed that he was the god of many things; judgment, precision, and divine insight into how the world worked. Now he seemed muddled, unsure of the future, distrustful of the instincts that had brought him so much success. No longer divine, he was simply a human being who had made his share of mistakes, ones he had inherited and others that he had fallen into all by himself. I felt an empathy for him that I had never felt before.

"There was never any confusion between my body and yours," Dad said, pressing back. "You were small. You were slight. You needed a push forward, toward growth. Toward energy and structure. You needed to learn what hustle was. What need was. That is what a father is supposed to teach. Why are you so ungenerous? Is it so difficult for you to accept my help?"

"Doesn't it depend on the form it takes? Pushing me to do what I wasn't ready for is a strange form of help. I was fourteen when you sent me to that girl, and she wasn't just some celebratory rite of passage, was she? She had a specific purpose. She was an agent. An agent to cure me of exactly what I'm not sure. Couldn't you have given me the chance to cure myself if that is what I thought I needed? What was the rush? Couldn't it have waited until I was ready?"

"I did what any father would have done."

"Really? Did your father do for you what you did for me?"

"I don't want to talk about this anymore. This conversation is over. I'd just like to ask you to reflect on it some more when you're not so angry. Try and see it from my perspective. If you can, I think you'll feel differently about it. I was certainly not trying to hurt you. You misunderstood. I did my job. Now do yours and grow up already!"

He had never been so pleading and rash at the same time. For a minute, I was frozen in place after he left the room. Maybe he was right. Maybe that was exactly what I needed to do, but I had a hunch that I had already done most of it.

I went up to my room and gathered my books and clothes in a jumble and threw them into my backpack. I was ready to leave my home behind me, its comforts as much as its anguish. Then I called a taxi, and when I sat on the crinkly backseat headed to the Ossining train station, I felt a dynamic element inside me, a harmonious combination of lightness and weight that was as new to me as my liberated body had felt the day before.

# chapter 20

In the basement of the Federal-style building where most of our classes were held there were three sprawling rooms. The front room, half below ground, housed hundreds of tiny mailboxes, one for each student. I checked mine every morning if for no other reason than to yank out the *Wall Street Journal*, to which my father had given me a subscription. I extracted it as discreetly as I could, given how completely it clogged the small box, and then started to fold it between my books so no one would see it. Nothing would have been as embarrassing at St. John's as being identified as a student who read the official record of big business and industry. And yet this morning I paused, still holding the paper.

It was spring, junior year. During the two years since our argument, Dad and I hadn't spoken much, broadening the gulf between us. When he began sending me the paper, I accepted it as a peace offering. In the meantime, he had sold his business. I watched from a distance how, as an employee of the new company, not an owner, he lost his autonomy and his direction. Danny reported that Adnan had vanished long before, and no one mentioned his name. Svetlana occasionally appeared in her blond swirled hairdo at the breakfast table, and Teddy roared up the driveway on his Triumph motorcycle, spraying gravel across the front circle onto the grass beneath the crab apple tree. Avoiding them was easy. They were eager to steer clear of me, too, so there was little chance of angry, prying questions slipping out of my mouth. But mostly I stayed away from home, since I had moved out of the dorms and rented an apartment on the top floor of a brown shingled house on Prince George Street.

At college, Daphne and Pat failed to return for the sophomore year. My freshman roommate, Roger, disappeared in the same way he'd arrived, without an explanation or leaving any trace. Bill was spread so thin between the Middleton Tavern, his camaraderie with the other waiters, and schoolwork that we never saw each other, and if we did we would nervously discuss that week's reading in not very much detail. In that way we skirted each other and the lingering questions of his involvement with Daphne.

The twice-a-week seminar readings absorbed most of my attention. Although I still didn't contribute much to the discussions, forcing out a sentence or two at most, I could feel some progress in my grasp of the material. By the time my class reached the Enlightenment, I discovered more than a few scattered passages where I felt confident I had understood what I had read and could participate in the evening's conversation.

That morning, as I snatched the *Journal* out of my box, I thought the room was empty and scanned the front page. Absentmindedly, I started reading an article in the middle column. It described small points of light being carried underground through thin cables that communicated with one another in an intelligent way. I was so engrossed that I didn't notice the few students sitting behind me, until their conversation distracted me from what I was reading. I heard the words *civilization* and *discontent* which told me they were seniors and discussing Freud. Their conversation had an easy bantering quality to it. They had been having this discussion and other ones like it for more than three years and knew how speak to one another without cutting in or belittling one another. It was easygoing, and I wanted badly to be part of a group like that.

This was how I first noticed Beatrice. Because the campus was small and there were fewer than five hundred students, I must have seen her before but couldn't remember when or where. She spoke quickly and kept combing her fingers through her brunette hair, sweeping it off her high brow and tugging it back over her head and to the side. All of her facial features were alert, her language incisive. She constructed sentences carefully, yet they sounded spontaneous. When she saw that I was staring at her, she motioned for me to join them. I tucked the *Journal* under my arm and sat in the big leather chair next to her.

"We're talking about Freud in case you're wondering. Reading *Civilization and Its Discontents* for tonight. This is our little warm-up.

You're a junior, right? You don't know what we're talking about, so let me get you up to speed. Freud is rehashing the Hobbes question. How do we as humans handle chaos? How do we accommodate the worst parts of our nature, and what does that mean to our communities. Hobbes believed that there had to be a sovereign to maintain order in society. Freud knew there wasn't one. Threats of violence and lust strain our civility. How can this tension be resolved in a civilized community? Does it have to be a source of anxiety? Is it our social fate to be in a state of permanent opposition to our human instincts?"

The others listened to her summary with interest but then slipped away one by one. We sat alone in the mailroom. The morning sun slanted low through the ground-level windows, and the strong light divided the small subterranean room into planes of light so that where we were sitting became a smaller space in which we were illuminated and alone. I felt as though I was in a trance, listening to her, mesmerized by the freckle patterns on her pale skin. Her large, light pink glasses didn't hide the animation in her eyes.

"So you've read Hobbes already. Do you think he's right? Do you think there's a sovereign who protects us from chaos and anarchy? Hold on a sec. What's your name? I'm Beatrice, but everyone calls me Bea. I know I've seen you around."

She had a tendency to ask a second or third question without letting me answer the first one. I didn't have time to say my name. "What do you think about Freud? I know you haven't read him yet, but you must have some ideas?" I was silent because I was thinking to myself how she had just given a shorthand version of my adolescent history. The tension she described was exactly the one my father imparted to Tim and me, whether we were ready for it or not. All of his sotto voce remarks about women who he pretended not to notice heightened it. His leering asides, his not-so-subtle evaluation of their bodies, his "spontaneous questions" about whether they had ever visited Tacoma, his appraisals of their "talent," were manifestations of a desire that he was barely able to stifle. We were mortified not because we didn't have some of those thoughts ourselves but because we didn't want to know that he had them, too. Each time he began his flirtations, we tried to distance ourselves from him, like little kids sticking their fingers in their ears to block out what they didn't want to hear.

"Most of us have given up on the sovereign idea, haven't we? Haven't you?" I managed to ask despite my distraction.

"Well, yes, but it's hard for me. My father is an orthopedic surgeon. He plays God. He manipulates people's bones and sets them back in place. His patients believe he is God. He is also the sovereign in our house. My mother is scared of him. She's a devout Catholic. She believes in his primacy and goes to church every day to pray. She knows the names and labors of all the saints. What religion are you?"

"I'm Jewish by birth but we barely celebrated any of the holidays. Maybe once a year. No bar mitzvah. Purely a cultural experience."

"Look, sorry, I have to go. What's your name again?"

"It's Jonathan, like the prince in the Old Testament," I said. "A son of King David."

"Oh, a prince! I wouldn't have guessed."

"My name is John Wellington Wells. I'm a dealer in magic and spells," I said, quoting McEnery. The memory came back violently, and I instantly regretted the reference.

"What's that?" she asked.

"Gilbert and Sullivan," I answered.

We stood up at the same time. I noticed that she was almost as tall as I was. Although I had always thought that the man should be taller than the woman, as my father was with my mother, I felt immediately comfortable next to her. With Daphne I had been acutely aware of my lack of stature. I walked out the door next to Bea, and our equal height felt like a pact between us. I could feel myself being drawn to her as if she were the unmoved mover Aristotle had described, the one I had been unable to find in Daphne.

As we had agreed we met up again that night at the Little Campus Inn after our seminars. Bea was sitting at the bar talking to a friend, but when I went over to her their conversation ceased instantly and she turned toward me. She had put on pink lipstick, and her hair was tied back. Over her jeans she wore a white dimpled blouse with missing fabric below her throat that framed an oval of skin. Through currents of alcohol and cigarettes stubbed out in the ashtray, I could smell her slight perfume, an ambrosial freshness. She was as animated as she had been that morning. Her eyes shone, her cheeks globed when she laughed and went smooth as she listened.

"How was your Freud?"

"Predictable," she said. "I just don't think that it's that bleak. I know the tension is there, but I can't feel it or don't want to. What about you?"

"It was our first *Critique of Pure Reason*. Not a good feeling."

"Do we have to talk about our books?" she asked me, and laughed. Her voice that was low splintered into a mix of registers, soprano with flinty notes.

"No, we don't. Kant gives me a headache, but I like the story of his leaving his house every day at exactly the same time and on the day he failed to appear, his neighbors knew he was dead. Do you think it's true?"

"I have *no* idea," she said. "How many girlfriends have you had? You're a city boy. You must have gone out with hundreds of girls."

"No, I'm not. I'm suburban. The only way I could go on a date was if my mother drove me. That only happened once."

"Who was she?"

"Her name was Polly. I met her in seventh grade in the dance class that they made us go to. She wore silver lipstick. I think that's why I fell for her."

"So you've had a lot of girlfriends, then."

"Many but only one. Polly doesn't count. We barely kissed. I was thirteen."

"What does that mean? That sounds like a saga. Do you want to tell me about it? I broke up with my boyfriend two months ago. We got sick of each other. No, that's not true. I got sick of him. But what does that mean, 'the many and the one'?" she asked again, lifting her chin toward me. I wanted to kiss her pink frosted lips so much more than I wanted to tell her how badly I had treated Daphne.

"Could I tell you another time? I promise you I will, but just not now. All right?"

"Sure. Whenever you're ready."

"Let's get out of here."

We stumbled out onto the uneven cobblestone street. I grabbed her hand before I realized I had done it and led her toward the campus. The outside stairs to my apartment lay between the Little Campus Inn and the college. As we got close to them, my legs started to buckle from the fear that I might repeat with Bea the mistakes I had made with Daphne. Panic spread through my joints, almost blocking my arms from sweeping her up and depositing her on one of the Indian rugs that carpeted my living room.

She stopped me as we walked and held my hand tightly. I knew she wanted me to kiss her by the way she paused and stared at me, and this time I was sure that I wouldn't stop myself. When I put my arms around her, I was the one who felt protected. As soon as we kissed, I knew that she wasn't trying to steal my privacy from me. It was the opposite. I was filled out, enriched by her curiosity and affection. Our strength, the taste of her lips, her desire, amplified me, and I wanted to stay there with her more than I wanted to hide.

A week later Bea moved into my apartment on Prince George Street. I helped her carry her suitcases across campus and up the wooden stairs. I tried not to watch her as she hung up her clothes in the closet I had cleared out for her, but I saw her examining one of my shirts. She unbuttoned it and put it on. It fit her much better than it fit me.

That night we heated up grilled cheese sandwiches in my toaster oven and sat on my living room rugs. There weren't any chairs.

"So, do you want to tell me the story now?" she asked.

"Which one?"

"Come on, Jon. You know. The many and the one. Start with the one. It sounds easier."

"I went out with a girl when I was a freshman for a few weeks. It was a disaster. I was afraid of her and couldn't speak to her. I couldn't say anything, I was so knotted up. She was the first normal girlfriend I ever had."

"So if the other ones weren't normal, what were they?"

"Yes, I promised to tell you that. So when I was around twelve my Dad thought I was too skinny and started making me do exercises. Jumping jacks, push-ups, pull-ups, et cetera. When I didn't gain any weight he tried to get me to eat more. He stuffed me with food. Years of chocolate milkshakes, buttered bread, extra potatoes. I only really liked steak. Thin, medium-rare slices. I loved steak so much, my mother made me a steak costume for Halloween. I was the only T-bone in our neighborhood." I stopped there for a minute. I chuckled at the memory of wearing the white toque on my head that Mom had fashioned out of blank paper and the pinkish slabs of meat she had painted so meticulously between the white strips of fat.

"Go on," she said.

"When I was fourteen, I was still tiny. None of Dad's pushing me to eat or bulk up had worked, and I really wasn't too interested in his plans for me anyway. All of the doctors he sent me to couldn't do anything for me either. He interpreted my lack of interest in his programs as a rebellion at first, and then he decided that if I didn't want to build up my body, I must be queer, or a freak. That was unacceptable, so he came up with a plan to correct me. He said he wanted to introduce me to a girl he knew who was sweet and pretty and loved young boys. He asked me if I'd like to meet her. I didn't know she was a prostitute. I didn't even know what a prostitute was. It seemed like a good idea at first, and it was exciting, but afterward I had this shaky feeling that I had participated in a deranged conspiracy. Not telling Mom was part of the deal. And then he sent me again. It stopped before I came to college."

I had never told the story out loud before. It sounded so peculiar that I wanted to get as much of it out of me as I could without stopping. To steady myself I stared at the remaining half of my grilled cheese sandwich. Bea didn't say anything at first. I could feel her scrutinizing me and imagined all of the terrible reactions she might be having. I braced myself for her judgment, but the silence expanded until I was forced to look up. There were tears on her cheeks.

"Your father did that to you? How old were you again?"

"I had just turned fourteen, but I was more like a child."

"I'm so sorry for you. You poor boy," she said, and took the plate out of my hand and set it down beside her. She pulled me closer. "You must hate him. Don't you?"

"I'm not sure what I feel about it. I'm uncomfortable thinking about him. Is that hatred?"

"Not necessarily. But you must feel something?"

"I don't know what I feel. Can something be too complicated for one feeling?"

"Yes. Of course. All the time. You don't have to say anything. Didn't your mother protect you? That's what mothers are supposed to do."

"She didn't know. I didn't want to tell her and get one of her sermons about love and how each love is unique."

She reflected for a moment. "You *are* skinny. Your dad was right about that, but that's your body type and it has no correlation to sexuality. How big is your father?"

"My size, basically, but he's much heavier than I am."

"Well, that's normal. Everyone gains weight when they age. You will too. There's a term for body type called the 'body habitus' in the literature."

Although St. John's didn't have a premed program, I knew that Bea wanted to be a doctor and was preparing to take the medical school admission tests as soon as she graduated.

"You are a small-boned ectomorph, not a freak. There is a classification for your size, and I'd imagine that your parents are in the same category. You are not a freak, or at least you weren't until your dad tried to fix you. Ha! What a bizarre thing to do. I can't believe it!" she exclaimed. "That is one of the weirdest stories I have ever heard. You poor boy," she repeated, and hugged me.

"You mean I'm big enough to fit in the medical lexicon?"

"Yes, presh, you're in the books," she said. *Presh*, short for "precious," was one of her endearments. "You can't be an oddball if you're in the books, right? Who knows why your father was so obsessed with this. He was probably your size when he was your age. Maybe that's why he did all that stuff to you. Oh my God. I can't imagine. Were you scared? Did you know what was going to happen when he sent you to the prostitute?"

"I was too scared to be afraid, if you know what I mean. I wouldn't let myself think about it, but I must have been terrified." As I spoke I felt the queasiness that I remembered from the taxi ride up Madison Avenue to Ingrid's apartment, but then it began to lift. There was a new elasticity in my neck and chest and spine that made me feel that I had been unshackled from my harrowing experiences.

"So, how much do you weigh now?" she asked curiously but as if the answer didn't matter that much to her.

"I don't know. The last time I checked I was under a hundred pounds, but that was a few years ago."

"And you haven't checked since?"

I shook my head. I had thought of weighing myself from time to time but had avoided it when the actual moment came. I didn't have the courage to fall short again.

"Let's put you on the scale and get this over with."

She took my hand and pulled me toward the tiny bathroom. She'd brought a scale with her to my apartment, and I tried to get on it fully clothed, still wearing my shoes, anything that would augment what I feared the number would be.

"That's pathetic. Get undressed. Take everything off, including your socks. Let's see what you weigh completely naked. Come on. Let's go."

I had never weighed myself in front of another person who wasn't a doctor, and never naked, but she insisted. She nudged me to the scale. The needle swung wildly from 90 to 120 before settling. "A hundred and four pounds," Bea announced.

I was astonished. When had I crossed the threshold? How could I not have even noticed? She put her arms around me and hugged me, but she didn't know how momentous the number was for me. How could she? It was a figure that towered over me in neon like the

Hollywood sign, a destination that I had always dreamed of seeing with my own eyes and never thought I'd reach.

The next evening I called home to tell my parents the news. Mom picked up the phone. Her reaction was jubilant. "Come home this weekend. I want to see you and celebrate." I could hear her turn toward Dad to tell him the news. He grunted something in the background that I couldn't decipher. "Dad says, finally. He wants you to come home, too. Why don't you bring Bea with you? We'd love to meet her."

"Maybe," I said, and froze. Bea sat next to me, listening expectantly.

Introducing Bea into our home struck me as premature. We barely knew each other. I had no idea what she would make of my businessman father in his neo-hippie, New Age phase who had painted black spirals on his big toenails. What would she think of Teddy and Svetlana or the shifting assembly of other drifters who had taken up residence in our house?

When Bea was at class the next day, I called Mom and said that I would come home and bring Bea with me on one condition: there must be no guests, no strangers, no gurus. It was not negotiable, I said, using one of Dad's favorite terms. Not even one of them, I insisted. Mom agreed without hesitation or consultation. She said, "As long as I can see you and meet Bea, I don't want anyone else here either. I'm sick of all these people, Jon."

When I hung up the phone, a settled feeling came over me, as if something fundamental had changed in my life. The panic was gone. The fear of judgment was replaced by stillness and rest. I realized that I was in love with Bea. The notion spread through my body, and I could feel it reach into my thinnest places—the muscles in my upper arms that my father squeezed to check on their circumference and my shoulders, which he said were weak and hunched. I knew then that I was loveable without alteration. I had never recognized that feeling before. Bea's presence was proof that love was achievable, and that possibility meant that I could feel it and was capable of returning it. Then I became certain that I wanted to bring Bea home with me so I could show her off and myself, too.

A dim memory flashed of Dad taking Tim and me to Jones beach on the Atlantic Ocean. It was our first visit to the ocean. We had seen lake waves before but never bigger ones that had a curl. I was nine and Tim was seven. The noise of the surf and the waves' power intimidated us. Dad badgered us to come in the water with him and showed us how to hop over the surf, dive into the curl of the waves and ride them in to the shore. He put his blue nose plug on and dove into the first one that rose in front of him. Tim looked at me as if to say, Maybe we should give it a try, so we went into the frothing water inch by inch. Waves broke in front of us. I ducked into the first one and felt the turbulence bubble over my head. After it broke and then receded, I floated out with the undertow. Soon I realized that I was past where the waves were breaking and I could tell I was on the wrong side of them. I started to flail and swam toward the beach using anxious, rapid strokes. After each wave rose beneath me and carried me nearer, I tried to put my feet down to find my footing. Each time my toes searched for a solid bottom, there was nothing but more water. I thrashed forward and sank down again. My arms were getting tired, but I kept moving forward with small strokes and kicks. The next wave broke over my head and salt water went up my nose, but it nudged me closer. I felt for the bottom again, and that time my feet felt the rippled sand on the ocean floor. The relief was enormous. I was saved.

# chapter 21

As soon as we walked in the front door, Mom hugged Bea as if they had met each other before. Mom wasn't the one who worried me. When Dad came toward her I watched with hypervigilance. How long would he clasp her hand in his? Would he hug her? And for how long? The strategy that I devised during the drive was that I would count to five and if his arms were still around her on the last beat, I'd intervene. He approached and held her hand between his, giving her his warmest, most compassionate stare. He held it for one second too many, and I bumped against him to distract him. Releasing her hand, he looked at me as if I were an annoyance that had thrown him off his game.

Grabbing Bea, I led her on a tour of the house. In the living room I told her about the fires Tim and I lit each night after dinner and how we vied to see who would strike the match. I took her into the kitchen with its blue Delft tiles of windmills and bonneted maidens milking cows. Marianita and the elaborate meals she and Mom had slaved over came back to me. Then I led Bea down the hall to the breakfast room vacant of its recent guests and finally to the dining room where I had struggled night after night to finish what was on my plate. I was overwhelmed by the room's warmth, the painted black-and-gold chandelier against the golden walls and the views through the window. Just outside was the patio where we had dinner during the summer. There was nothing menacing about it. The wooden chairs with the straw matting looked inviting, as if they offered their occupants a chance for a leisurely conversation without rancor, a chance to debate a question of interest to everyone.

After that, Bea and I went outside in spite of the cold. There wasn't much to show her in late January, but I gave her the tour of the upper lawns and the lower ones, the rose garden and the rock gardens and the other ones Tim and I had spent hours and days setting up sprinklers for. The work that had been a burden years ago was now a source of pride. I had contributed to the beauty of the gardens and lawns. I looked at them with admiration and pleasure. We walked up the gravel path that went by the cabin, our adolescent refuge where Adnan had taken up temporary residence. The screened-in porch was deserted, the furniture stacked up for the winter.

That night we slept in separate bedrooms. After I turned out the lamp in my top bunk and the embers of the black-light posters began to glow as they still did inexplicably after so many years, I climbed down the ladder and felt my way around the old black recliner and the Ethan Allen desk that smelled of milled wood. I tiptoed through the bathroom that connected Tim's and my room to Danny's room, where Bea was sleeping in Danny's single bed. I lifted the covers, slipped in beside her, and held fast to her in the dark. She was the wall I wanted to hide behind. Although I had explained some of the past to her, I didn't think she could understand how sweet that moment was. I wasn't even sure that I could understand all of it myself.

The next day we had a quick lunch before driving back to Annapolis. Dad fixed his favorite weekend meal for himself, a sandwich of salami slices on challah bread. He only used one slice of bread because he said he knew he was getting paunchier and rubbed the bulge over his waistband. He called them open-faced sandwiches and said they came from the Scandinavian tradition. He claimed that two pieces of bread was a typical example of American overindulgence. The second one was completely unnecessary. He followed each bite of salami with an even bigger bite of a sour dill pickle.

When Bea followed Mom to the kitchen, Dad turned to me and asked if I would come upstairs for a moment. "There is something I want to show you."

"Why?" I asked suspiciously.

"Just follow me."

I trailed him up the main staircase, but instead of turning left to his bedroom, he took a quick right turn and opened the door to the attic. As I went up the rickety wood stairs, I could already smell the dampness and mothballs. It had been years since I'd been to the attic—a large rectangular room where we used to play on rainy days. The floor was covered in tumbling mats for practicing our somersaults. When I stepped on them, I felt unstable, as if I were tipsy. Without warning, Dad grabbed my arm and turned sideways in a semi-crouch.

"My brother, Paul, and I used to play a game when we were kids," he said. "We'd try and sock each other in the arm as softly as we could. We'd do that for a while back and forth, and then one of us would hit the other as hard as he could and that was the end of the game. So do you want to try it? We can skip the early rounds."

"Is that what you wanted to show me? Tim and I used to do that too. All the kids at Adams did. You want to punch me as hard as you can? Why?" I asked.

"No, I want you to punch me. I want to see how strong you got. Come on. I haven't felt your muscles in a long time. For old times' sake. You have a girlfriend now, don't you?"

"What's that got to do with it?"

"Everything. And not hard to look at, either. So will you or won't you?"

"I don't want to."

"Come on, Jon. You're not going to hurt me no matter how hard you hit me," he said, stretching his upper lip over his teeth as if he were about to shave it. He clenched his right arm against his ribs. I turned sideways into what I thought was a boxing stance and tapped his arm with my fist.

"No! I said as hard as you can, not as light as you can. More macho! Show me you can defend yourself. And her. I need to know. You won't hurt me. I've done this hundreds of times. Come on. Come on already," he said, taunting.

Feeling my blood burst into my neck and shoulders, I hit him as hard as I could in the middle of his arm. I could have sworn I felt solid bone beneath the muscle and flesh. He winced and released a dramatic breath, then gave me a look of acknowledgment that said *Now we are even.* It was time for us to think about new things: the future, adult life. With one punch, the past could be severed like an island from the mainland, surviving in a remote, tranquil setting without greater scrutiny.

"Not bad," he said, shaking out his arm. "Not bad at all. We're done. Now we can rejoin the ladies."

# epilogue

On a Saturday morning many years later, my wife, Juanita, and I invited Dad to spend the weekend with us at our home in Connecticut on a little river. After college Bea had gone to medical school, married a doctor, and moved south. By that time, Juanita and I had four children. It was always difficult to include Dad in the family's swirl of activities, but perched on a couch on the back deck of the house, he was mostly content to watch his grandchildren as they played.

The house we had grown up in had been sold. Mom and Dad had divorced years before, and she had remarried, living nearby with her new husband. Dad lived in a shaky urban solitariness that included various hopeless relationships and was watched over by a housekeeper as his health faltered. He had been seriously ill from random events: listeria that he had caught from a spoiled piece of cheese, cerebral meningitis that made him lose most of his short-term memory, and an unexplained case of internal bleeding that was so severe that all his children had to donate blood to stabilize him. He had mostly recovered from these crises, but he had gained almost a hundred pounds. "Eating is the only pleasure I have left," he explained candidly in answer to a question I hadn't asked.

Andrew, my eldest son, said he'd like to come with me to the station to pick Dad up. Waiting for him in the parking lot took patience because he was usually the last person off the train. When we spotted him we waved our arms and he walked toward us slowly, rocking from one bowed leg to another. His breathing was shallow from chronic asthma, and he fumbled with the inhaler that he puffed on constantly. When he reached us he leaned over and gave Andrew a hug, then shook my hand.

After dinner I helped him change into his pajamas and laid out the pills he was prescribed to take before bedtime. If we didn't watch him carefully, he would hide them in his pocket or simply forget to take them. Then I maneuvered him onto the bed and handed him his travel bag emblazoned with the emblem of the now defunct Pan Am, which he liked to keep next to him. He never took off the plated gold necklace that had the #1 icon on it and got tangled in the folds of skin around his neck. He wore it, he claimed, so that he would never forget who he was or what priority his goals held for him. When I hugged him, he squeezed my wrist to make sure I heard him, and said in a confidential tone, "Jon, you know, I'm going to live to be a hundred?"

It was a statement, not a question. I nodded. He had told me this many times before, and yet whenever we said good night, I was never sure that he would be alive in the morning. That night I woke up at 4 A.M., disoriented and sweating. Suddenly I realized that there would be no better moment to ask him about the past. I forced myself to get up.

When I walked into his bedroom downstairs, he was turned away from me on his side. His snoring made a back-and-forth sound like a saw cutting through hardwood. He gulped for air and tensed as I sat on the edge of his bed. Sensing that someone had intruded on his sleep, he turned toward me deliberately.

"Dad," I said. "I need to talk to you." He twitched and stirred. "Dad, I need to talk to you," I said again, and squeezed his hand.

"What?" he said. "What is it? What's wrong?"

"I need to ask you a question. Think back thirty years ago. I was a boy around fourteen years old. Are you with me?" I asked him. He nodded groggily, trying to follow me. "That was when you sent me to a prostitute. Do you remember why you did that?"

"What?" he said. "What are you talking about? I never did that."

"Yes, you did."

"You must be thinking of somebody else. It wasn't me." His voice was slurred from sleep.

"No, it was definitely you. You gave me the money and the address and set it up for me. I came to your office in the Pan Am Building, remember? What made you do it?" I asked.

"What are you saying?" he asked me, more muddled than annoyed.

"Did you send me because you were worried about my weight? Or because you thought I might be gay and you wanted to straighten me out? Or did you just think that was the right thing for a father to do? Why didn't you send Tim or Danny?" I asked, giving him a range of options.

"I never thought you were gay. Didn't you have a girlfriend back then? So I guess you weren't, were you?" he answered.

Holding his hand, I paused, thinking that he might need more context to remember. "When I was fourteen I was in my last year at Adams and a teacher was picking on me. Do you remember the fat Latin teacher McEnery who sat on me and squished me? Were you trying to protect me from him or some of the other bullies there? Are you sure you don't remember it? You made the appointment for me and gave me a hundred-dollar bill. Did you think that sending me to her would keep me safe? Are you sure you don't remember that?"

"I'm positive." He shook his head. "As positive as I am of anything."

"Well, do you remember worrying about how thin I was? You made me chocolate milkshakes and forced me to do countless exercises. Chin-ups. Push-ups. Jumping jacks. Do you remember the crazy doctors you took me to who said I needed growth hormones?"

"Jon, I'm sorry, but I just don't remember any of that. It's all gone. A blank. I was thin too at your age."

"I know you were. You showed us the pictures. So what gave you the idea to do that to me?" I asked again.

"Do what?" he asked.

"Send me to hookers."

"You can say it as many times as you like, but that won't make me remember what I can't remember." There was a brief pause that I took to mean that he was fishing through his garbled mind for it. "If you say it happened, then I believe you, okay? Let's go back to sleep." A note of irritation crept into his voice.

Then I realized that there was nothing more to say. There was no further revelation, and there never would be. Elements of the truth, theories, motivations, and other figments might arise or vanish, but the only person who could verify them was unable or unwilling. I gave his hand a squeeze. "Pleasant dreams," he said, as he always did when he stayed with us, and turned away from me.

I sat down in the living room and looked at the river. The moonlight was shining on it through the leaves. I thought of the memory of that harrowing time as a powerful city that had once been the capital of an empire. It had derived its authority from conquest, not enlightenment or justice. Now it was abandoned but still standing in the middle of nowhere. There were no children or dogs playing in its courtyards. All life was vanquished. The ruins that remained didn't inspire fear. There was no visceral power remaining that could destroy anything or threaten anyone. It had lost its ability to wage war and tyrannize and had no other values to redeem it. Its triumphs and defeats, the intimidation of its force, its random cruelty and rashness and the despair that came in its wake, were gone. All that was left were crumbled walls and turrets, the half-salvaged memory of its realm.

The little bits of moonlight that fell on the river were more real than the sting of those distant events. Time doesn't heal anything, but time undoes what was built. It tugs at the supporting beams and rots them. It bends the nails. Gravity asserts itself. It dismantles, and when it is done only a souvenir is left behind.

The effect of time is a partial, involuntary forgiveness. What Dad had done hadn't been undone, but the wound had grown over and what was left was a vague sorrow; sorrow for him who felt it must be done and bewilderment at the ways in which I had struggled to overcome its effects.

There was a kind of peace in the ruins of the city—an arid, empty peace but peace nonetheless. And in that place of rest that had been reached only after challenges and quests, I was surrounded by the vibrancy of new life that I played a part in nurturing and letting thrive. My children could benefit from the wisdom my experience had given me and learn from what I had learned about self-respect and respect for others. Or maybe they would know it by themselves, instinctively, and without taking a hand in it, I could watch it unfold with love and awe.

# acknowledgments

Thank you to Michael Zilkha at Ze Books for his steadfast belief in this book. I am grateful to Chris Heiser at Unnamed Press for his meticulous editorial help and insight. Thanks to Kelsey Nolan at Ze Books for her involvement and to Olivia Taylor Smith at Unnamed Press. In addition, I am thankful for the patient help of Pamela Malpas and Lucinda Karter at the Jennifer Lyons Agency.

Without the attention and encouragement of Elisa Petrini this book would not have reached its current form. Her persistence and stamina were invaluable.

Thanks to the many readers of this manuscript from its early to its late stages including Scott Lasser, Derek Green, Betsy Bonner, Karen Glenn, Christopher Merrill, David St. John, Lucas Wittmann, Martha Rhodes, Vicki Riskin, Laure de Gramont, Rebecca Jordan, Laura Dail, Cate Marvin, John Deming, Michael Corbett, James Truman, Tobias Wolff, Roger Cohen, Bill Clegg, Allen Kurzweil, Adrienne Brodeur and many others.

I am grateful to my family members who had the patience to read all or parts of this to advise and correct, especially Jane Wells, Tom Wells, Alice Wells, David Wells and Beth Wells.

And, finally, I appreciate that my kids have given me the time and space to get this right: Alexander, Juliet, Delilah and Gabriel.

**Jonathan Wells** has published three poetry collections with Four Way Books: *Debris*, *Train Dance*, and *The Man with Many Pens*. His poems have appeared in The New Yorker, Ploughshares, AGNI, the Academy of American Poets Poem-a-Day series, and many other journals. *The Skinny* is his first book of prose.

@ZEBooks_USA

www.facebook.com/zebooksusa

@zebooks_usa

www.zebooks.com

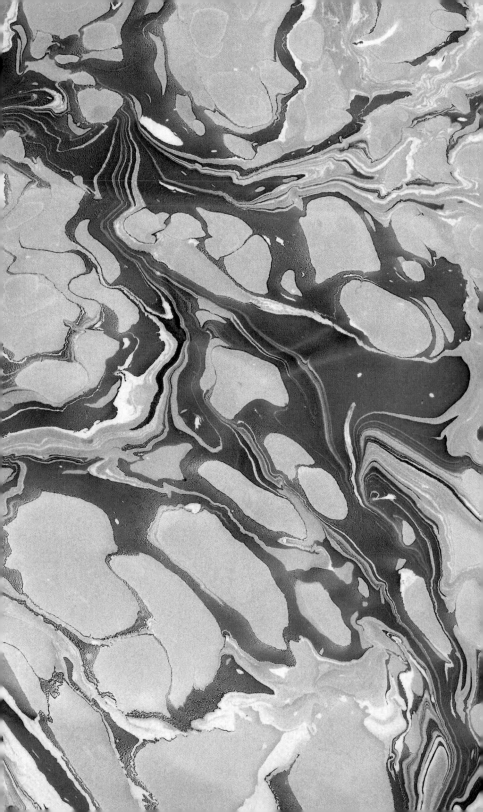